With Radical Faith and Effortless Grace

The Journey to Heart Space

Julie Jacobs

With Radical Faith and Effortless Grace
The Journey to Heart Space

Copyright ©2010 by Julie Jacobs

No portion of this work may be reproduced or transmitted in any form or by any means, electronic or mechanical, including photocopying and recording, or by an information storage or retrieval system, without written permission from Julie Jacobs.

First Edition

Indigo Moon Publishing
Portland, OR

Cover artwork by Kim McElroy
Book cover, interior design and layout by Bruce Conway

Printed in the U.S.A. on recycled paper

Library of Congress Control Number: 2010902947

$16.95

ISBN: 978-0-615-35785-0

Dedication:
To you Anamchara – Mi corazon besa tu alma.

Author's Acknowledgements:
With Radical Faith and Effortless Grace...
The Journey to Heart Space

Filled with gratitude and humility I wish to thank those that agreed to take this journey with me, whether they knew they were taking it or not. To my beautiful children.. You are the reason for the journey in the first place – I love you both more than words can say. I am honored and proud to be your Mother. To my Mothers, the one who chose to give me life and the one who chose to help me live it. You are my rocks of strength, courage and grace. I am who I am because of you. To you Momma June, all my love. What you have given, and continue to give does not go un-noticed or unappreciated – this journey would not have been possible without you. Thank you. To my parents together, I am truly grateful for the unwavering support in every one of my adventures, it appears I had a method to the madness after all. Thank you for your faith in me when I didn't have it inside of myself, it is in that faith that all things became possible. To my lifeboat sisters, Kelley King and Michelle Watson... Wow, what a ride. For your wisdom, laughter and grace notes along the way I am forever grateful. And I can't wait to see what the universe has in store for us next ☺ To my life coach Nancy Nixon, thank you can not convey the place I hold for you, in so many ways this story is possible because of the work we've done together.

To the Seer, Diane Caldwell... your compassion, light and wisdom is a true gift. I am very blessed to be able to move into my light, as a result of learning from yours. And to you Chelle, the journey is still moving forward. Thank you for what feels like an entire life of friendship. Thank you for reading, re-reading and the hours and hours of conversation that has led me to this place. To you Dixie, my amazing four-legged soul sister. I am different and better for having loved you. To the students of the Public Service Career Foundations class, August 2009, what an amazing group, I am so honored that I got to spend time teaching, learning and growing with you. I learned far more from you than you know. This is what happens when you are; willing to say yes and you believe it's possible. Much gratitude and compassion to you and to the roads you have chosen to travel. Kim McElroy, you are a light. Thank you for believing in me and making this possible under what appeared to be impossible timelines. It is as if it was always meant to be. I couldn't be more honored to have your work so beautifully convey mine. In the end, the greatest gift of all is your gift of friendship, I am honored. And to you Anamchara. wherever the journey finds you. It is as it was always intended to be.

Prologue…

This is my side of the story, the story that my soul is begging to tell in quiet whispers. It is the story of the past, a past so distant that it has origins in other lifetimes. It is the story of the present and of the gifts of wisdom and life lessons I learned in the embrace of a soul mate that came to lead me to discover the keys of my own kingdom. He held the keys to the kingdom of my heart and the quiet knowing of my own Divine Truth. But as in every journey, at least the ones that hold significant passion and promise, the current that moves through the human River of Life can become treacherous and full of detours along the way. It is in the lessons I learned navigating the River with him that I am forever changed. It is in all the moments that I could see the reflection of where I had been and who I had become at the water's edge that held the possibility, for me, of transformation.

Alone and isolated in my lifeboat on the River of Life I cast about aimlessly in the current, as it drifted through twists and turns of every opportunity I had to learn the life lessons I had come to this human place to learn. Desperately fighting for control I struggled and fought, careening recklessly between one hidden boulder after another as they built in size and number that led to the waterfall that was before me. As the water turned crystalline clear I could see in its reflection the characters in the story that were asking to come aboard. Some were wise, compassionate and full of love. Others carried with them the darkness and fear of traveling to an unknown destination, a place inside of me that I had never known existed. It was a place that offered me the possibility to stop and to learn and if I chose to be brave enough to trust what was happening, would lead me to reflection, redemption and resurrection. Each of the characters who chose to join me on these pages had a purpose and a story to tell. The characters are alive in us all. Can you find them in the reflection of the mirror I hold for you? The time has come. We're about to push away from the shore. As I sent over the rope of acceptance for the journey, one by one they came aboard.

The first to arrive was clad in black-heeled spiked boots and skin tight leather leggings that held the talons of her dark and controlling power. It was the Witch – the one who at the beginnings of this tale held me unconscious in her captivity. The Wicked Ego Witch had a sensuous dark magic that held an allure that was all consuming, provocative and powerful. Ahh, I knew her so well. Tall and fierce she exuded a raw ferocious beauty. Blonde spikes of short hair sprung up all around her almost cherubic face. She possessed hypnotic almond shaped brown eyes the color of chocolate and lips so full of passionate lies that I would hang on her every word, taking her ranting as the gospel for which I lived my life. She took every opportunity to jump immediately to false assumptions with her loud obnoxious lies of inadequacy, fear, pride, anger and greed.

Without warning, her sinuous, leather-covered arm snaked out to elbow her way to the top of my passenger manifest shoving me out of the helm of my lifeboat. That was just our way. She'd been in control of my life, my brain and my heart for so long that it just seemed natural to witness her outrageous behavior. I moved aside, handed over the paddles and prayed that she knew enough to get us safely through whatever was coming ahead. In the clasp of her ruby red fingernails she held a small dark figurine. As she elbowed me to the side, the figurine fell to the floor of the boat. It was a Dark Horse. In a burst of greed and anger she snatched up the Dark Horse, but just as the figurine disappeared into her bag of black magic, I felt a wave of light and hope.

The next one to find her way to me was Radical Faith. She burst through the surface of the clear blue water with her sword poised high above her. At its hilt was a bejeweled symbol that seemed faintly familiar to me, a gold cross at its center surrounded at each end with magnificent heart shaped rubies. Scattered glints of green emeralds formed a Celtic braid connected at each end by four cornered rubies. In diamonds, an anchor was nestled deep in the center of the jewel encrusted scabbard. As her sword rose up from the darkness of what lay below, her graceful hand reached up to take hold of mine. As our hands connected I feel a jolt of hope wind its way up through the center of my soul. Her presence was radiant, strong and steadfast. She towered above me in her long flowing cape of gold that surrounded her powerful and lithe feminine figure. Clothed in riding breeches and a carefully draped tunic, she was belted at the waist in knots of gold. Her hair surrounded her head like a halo of auburn, cascading down her back in ripples and curls. In the depth of her royal blue eyes I found a strength and reserve that filled me with the courage I would need to continue on.

Sensing the ripples of change on the water's surface the Wicked Ego Witch wheeled around and stepped so far back that she threatened to go overboard completely. Shoving her black heeled boot into the center of my life raft, she righted herself with a ramrod stiffening as she took back control of the helm without saying a word. Radical Faith simply smiled and sheathed her sword as she settled in for the long journey ahead.

A radiant burst of sunlight poured through a break in the thunderous sky. In its luminous reflection, the last passenger for this journey came down through the center of the divine rays of light. Effortless Grace caught the tendrils of a beautiful breeze and shield in hand touched her beautiful golden foot down in the middle of my lifeboat. At the center of her shield, was the same jeweled symbol – of love, faith and hope. Her long, gorgeous, jet black hair fell almost straight to the ground, and her turquoise blue eyes held a peace so profound I felt surrounded in the depth of their pools. Simply dressed, in cascades of gold, she shimmered with an iridescence that was simple and so unadorned that its majesty and truth needed no further explanation. Standing next to her sister, Radical Faith, they shone together with a peaceful wisdom that was so captivating all I could do was simply gaze at them in quiet reflection. I'd never allowed such beauty so close to me before, close enough to share a journey through a waterfall of epic proportions.

Surrounded by the sisters I felt safe and protected. They would have much to teach me if I could find the courage to share the journey they offered. Effortless Grace parted her delicate lips and as if speaking as the breath of Life said, "Sister, we join you now. Your Other, the Anamchara is nearing – you can see him there, just in the reflection of the distance. Trust the process, trust yourself. You have all that you need." "But wait," I said, "I don't understand what you mean. What is an Anamchara?" "Anamchara is your soul friend. He was brought to you in this time to help you learn your lessons. With your Anamchara you will share the deepest recesses of your soul. You will be able to see yourself through his reflection. Have Faith. Trust what is about to unfold. Trust him to be the reflection of what you need to see. The time has come."

As the pull of the River moved us closer and closer I saw him, the one who was to be Anamchara. Our eyes locked together in a space of all knowing as he threw his rope of relationship out for me to grab. Scattered in his boat were his very own cast of characters with their own stories and significance to the journey. Catching my eye was another small dark figurine. There she was again, the Dark Horse. What was her significance to us both? Tethered together, the Anamchara and I looked deeply into each other's eyes as the roar of the waterfall became a deafening rally cry to what lay ahead.

My One…

When the Anamchara of my heart crashed upon my shore, I had no choice but to accept the invitation to take the journey that he beckoned with his very soul. The music in my heart to live again was so powerful that I had no choice. The melody was ethereal and haunting and it teased and lingered in its dance as the winds of change and growth in this lifetime whispered and tempted to soften the edges of my ragged and battle weary heart. As he began to sing his heart song of possibility, I could feel in the song its gentle insistence begging me with mysticism and lyric, to be brave enough to follow the rhythm and trust in its flow.

That we had shared this journey before in another time and place is the only explanation, the only thing that makes any sense to explain why I would have accepted the heart song of this Anamchara man. The connection we shared was larger than us both, it begged of healing and growth if only we would be brave enough to trust in what was about to unfold before us. In the beginning I did not, I tried to stay neutral I tried to stay safe and sovereign. When our journey began, I didn't know of the lessons that would be revealed to me in the mirror of his reflection.

It was nearing Thanksgiving, and I felt a faint rumbling in my soul to take the next step towards relationship, at least in theory anyway. I had been single for so long, so lost, so empty and unfeeling that in retrospect it is comedic irony. I had built my fortress of solitude around single motherhood and the bustling cacophony of raising my children. There is nothing easy about learning to navigate a relationship particularly when the truth of the matter is that you don't believe you have any concepts or skills to navigate one. I staged my war of solitude on the premise that I didn't have the time, energy or any emotion left to give. Being a single mother, sole provider and Jill of all trades had taken anything I might have had to offer to another. At least that's what I told myself. It was a clever stage trap of lies I had built inside my own head to stay out of the River of Life that leads to Heart Space, the open flowing current through the river that is pure love. It was not only the love that I was saving for my Other, but love for every living thing around me. This decision to wall myself off from the possibility of love had repercussions in every aspect of my life. It was safe on my shore all alone. I remained firmly planted in the sand as the distractions of men who could never quite measure up tried to come ashore. Sometimes I would let them, welcoming the respite they offered me with the possibility of not quite being so alone in my journey. I was always hopeful in my conquests, however misplaced, based on the thread of truth they all shared in their broken loveless-ness for themselves first, and then in their inability to love another. None of these men had any more to give than I did. Our dances in relationship were short lived and ill-fated from the beginning. It was the only dance I knew how to do. Eventually I just gave up entirely to face my journey alone in the shell of human existence I had created.

I said to the Universe in a moment of prayer that I was ready. It was time for, "My One." I've come to learn that the Universe will always answer, absolutely always. I had no idea whatsoever what I was asking for, maybe I was hoping that whoever showed up would be the next distraction in the long line of many that had come before the Anamchara. When he crashed upon my shore and threw down the gauntlet to venture away from my safety and journey into the River of Love, I was powerless against the pull of his tide.

About a week after I had staked my claim in a moment of prayer, I renewed a membership to an online dating service that had been successful for me in earlier years. I didn't change one single piece of information about myself or my life, nor did I update any photos contained in the post. Floods of "potential matches" came across my email, and I glanced at them with mixed amusement. None particularly caught my attention, except for one. The name alone on the post was enough for me to take a mildly interested glance at his profile.

What he wrote was so intense and emotional, his words so wildly provocative and so eloquent that my little girl fantasy of her perfect Prince Charming stood up and started, screaming, "pick him, pick him." I got goose bumps as his words floated and danced across the screen and tickled my senses with their power and promise. I could feel through his writing the passion, the raw power, his vision and his dreams. A man who could write like that? And there the fantasy of who he might be started to take form and shape in my imagination.

Just when my interest was piqued in its intensity, the door slammed shut. When I finished reading his profile, I thought that there was just simply no way I was going to open the door to that possibility. He seemed too real, his emotion and passion too overwhelming. Perhaps it was the intensity and power that I felt through his words that stirred up something deep inside me, something primal and instinctive, the very thing I had abandoned for myself so long ago. How could I possibly measure up to the potential and promise I felt through his words? I did the only thing I knew how to do in that moment; I simply walked away.

Several days later, I received an introductory email from the man I had avoided. Intrigued and curious, but safe in my cyberspace domain I answered him. We went through the prescribed process of sending each other questions back and forth. For some reason one day I just quit answering. There was no reason; I just stopped. Or maybe there was a reason, one I was so unconscious of that the ripple didn't even register against the sand of my abandoned and desolate shore.

He sent one last email to try to re-engage my interest. His email was titled "Mi Alma, Where For Art Thou and more Temporate." I had no clue what 'mi alma' meant at the time but I opened the email anyway. He went on to say that he enjoyed our communication and wanted to put out one more effort. He thought that I seemed to possess a level of substance that was missing in most of his other matches. The sentence that got me was, "If either one of us chooses to end communication we can do so without drama or delay." He didn't have me at hello, but shortly thereafter, with one sentence I became engaged in the game. It seemed he offered a safe and guaranteed promise that either of us could walk away at any time without the drama usual in relationships. Hell, I was walking dead and not feeling emotion anyway so that was as close to a guarantee as I could get. The journey with Anamchara had basically started at "Goodbye."

He had asked me a series of questions about my life, my work, my children and animals. I was only too eager to share. I responded with a rambling and reflective email about my life and the usual details of being a single working mother. For some odd reason I started writing about my Ranch. I started the first sentence to that email by saying I felt describing my Ranch might have some "long term relevance." I wrote about the magical nature of my former property and of the spirit and peace that I had found there. One of the qualities that attracted me to him in the beginning was his life work and the fact that he owned a large acreage property, very similar to the one I had so recently lost. Anamchara seemed to be a very driven man, on a quest to build his personal vision. I was intrigued and I wanted to know more.

We quickly moved over to the world of being real to

each other. It was now Christmas and I remember vividly the blizzard that had blanketed our city. We were paralyzed in the tranquil and dangerous beauty of a winter storm that was unrelenting in its wave after wave of snow and ice. The city was shut down as the clock to Christmas Eve was fast approaching. I remember the champagne colored twinkling of the Christmas tree lights as I waited for his phone call for the very first time. My mind spun wildly with the possibilities of who and what he might really be. Would I resonate with the sound of his voice? Would we have anything to say to each other? More importantly, would the dance of getting to know each other find its own natural rhythm and flow? My imagination had built him up to be every answer to every fairy tale I'd ever read – every dream of "happily ever after" I had ever hoped for. As the minutes ticked away, very true to my own rhythm of things I couldn't wait any longer. I finally picked up the phone and called him first, patience never being one of my stronger virtues.

I wish I could say I had every sentence of every conversation memorized, but I don't. I remember the easy flow and the natural rhythm of two people trying to get a sense of each other. One conversation turned into another – always filled with marvelous stories. He was an incredible story teller. I would become so captivated on those nights stretched out between the magical twinkling Christmas tree lights and the crackling persistence of the fireplace that I would literally get lost in time. We'd talk for hours, telling stories both real and imagined. He led me on the journey through my mind and captured me there – at least that part of me.

The phone rang fairly early one night and he said, "I'll be there in a couple hours, will you go out to dinner with me?" I was absolutely floored. It was a spontaneous and beautiful invitation, but it was already nightfall in the middle of the three worst weeks of blizzard our city had ever known. Using the foul weather as an excuse, I side stepped the invitation and asked if we could postpone to the next day. He had caught me completely off guard with his spontaneous invitation. I could have gotten ready and gone to meet him, but somewhere in the back of my mind thoughts trickled through about being inadequate, about not having the time to put on the mask of perfection that I tried so desperately to hide behind. Perhaps it was just plain fear. The conversations I'd had with him to this point were filled with passionate intensity, not the physical kind, but the kind you feel with someone who is alive and on fire in his life. He was wildly attractive to me, almost like a drug. I wanted to know how to find that fire again inside of myself, the life fire I'd practically extinguished altogether. During the phone calls we'd had to this point he would dig deep and call on me to answer those deeply personal questions about myself, a place most fear to tread. I thrived on the chance to go to those places, the places that no one had been brave enough to ask about before. The acknowledgement of my own inner depth and substance was an aphrodisiac to my soul. He offered me the invitation to step into my own fire, breathe my own Truth and simply be. Perhaps my reluctance to meet him at his first spontaneous request was simply about the possibility that the reality of who he was, alive, living, breathing and in front of me wouldn't live up to who I needed him to be.

My reticence was short lived as I proposed a dinner meeting for the next night. I guess I believed that with enough advanced notice I could get my Wicked Ego Witch under control to suck up enough courage to face the truth of this man. Of course, at the time I didn't know it was she, the Wicked Ego Witch, who was so in control of my mental ruminations – we hadn't yet been formally introduced. She was embedded in my every thought and controlled much of my every move. She may have been smoky and dark, but she was so alluring in her words of failure, shame and blame that I couldn't yet distinguish her truth from my own. Like it or not, the time had come to launch my lifeboat into the River of Relationship, again.

Anamchara and I didn't live in the same city, which is either a blessing or a curse depending on where we were in the journey, but since this was still the beginning the distance was a blessing. As an independent woman who was always in total control of her life, I got to make all the plans for our first meeting. This tiny little bit of control gave me a sliver of safety and comfort to gently push my lifeboat away from the shore.

I got to the restaurant early, because I am always early. The only rational thought going through my mind was alcohol. My nerves were banded tightly together and I felt frozen with trepidation as I went into the bar and slugged back in rapid succession two glasses of wine. While I was there, playing softly over the Musak was a jazz version of the only song in the world that reminded me of the last man I had really truly loved. Our first date had been at this very place. I'm still not sure why I chose this restaurant perhaps it was the ambiance that lends itself so beautifully to meeting someone for the very first time. The coincidence of the music peeked into my conscious for a brief flicker and disappeared as quickly as it'd been realized. The clock was still ticking, and my Anamchara was about to arrive.

Because he was always late, and always lost, it took awhile. I walked out to the parking lot to meet him and cell phone to cell phone heard his response to the first time he ever saw me. "God you are gorgeous," was all that he said. Our first moment, to me, was completely surreal. He was a very unusual man in both looks and intensity, his presence was so much larger than his stature. His eyes penetrated to the very depths of my soul – and that was at our first hello.

Anamchara is disabled or other-abled or whatever politically correct terminology is used not to offend those that walk through this world in a physical body that has challenges. The truth of his difference is relatively insignificant, or so I had hoped prior to our meeting, but as the theoretical moment turned into the reality of the moment, I wasn't so sure. He was a beautiful man. His hair was wild, and despite his best efforts to control his unruly curls, they sprang to life to match his passionate nature. His smile was contagious and his energy magnetic. He radiated love. He radiated the open hearted, compassionate space of safe emotional expression... something I had never experienced before. There was a genuine-ness of spirit about him that immediately made me feel a sense of emotional safety and put me completely at ease.

He was a man who took physical control of his situation through a cocky swagger and intimidating physical stance. Five seconds after meeting him I forgot completely that he walked through his world with physical limitations. As I was taking his physical truth all in, he lifted his arm to envelope mine, and we walked into the restaurant. Our conversation flowed easily, and the food was spectacular. In one sense it was like I had known him my entire life, maybe even longer but in the other, he was a complete mystery. He was a stranger with a strange hold over me that was yet to be determined. The Anamchara of my heart has a story to tell, and that story is his own but in that story carries the threads of a tragedy that would shape and mold him for the rest of his life.

I finally got around to asking him to tell me his story and his answer, shook me to the core, a place that had been so recently revealed to me, that its coincidence could not be overlooked, even in the moment. We shared the experience of being forever changed by electricity, for me in another lifetime, for him, in this one. There was a paralyzing moment of pure truth and knowing of this person as I felt frozen in time.

The Door and the Keys…

I didn't know when this journey began that for some time before it started, I was being given keys along the way to help me unlock the mystery contained in the journey that was about to unfold. Sometimes those keys showed up as people, sometimes the keys showed up in a paragraph in a book, sometimes those keys showed up as experiences that threatened to topple the tenuous foundation of core values and beliefs I had held on to so tightly.

I've always had a questioning mind. To accept a "truth" at face value seemed to me to be fraught with ignorance and this included traditional pillars of religious thought. I am devoutly spiritual, that foundation I have never questioned, but being raised as the daughter of a man of the cloth, I had plenty of opportunity to see the difference between Sunday morning rhetoric and the reality of the rest of the week. I guess it is what seemed to me to be pretense, always struck me as wrong. Live what you believe. That's a challenge I extend to every human being of every race, creed and religion in our human world. For me it seemed quite simple, every religion and spiritual tradition – those of the light that stand in Christ-consciousness have the same message. At the core of every tradition are the exact same principles. How then is one belief right and another wrong? How then do we stand so firmly in our own rhetoric and beliefs that we can go to war to prove our rightness?

There has always seemed to me to be more, a Universal Truth of peace, love, compassion and grace, a truth that begins with Self. My journey to universal Truth and myself started with the Seer and a long time before Anamchara crashed onto my shore.

This universal Truth, and particularly as I've come to truly know, and more importantly live its existence, has been talked about and practiced for centuries. Buddhism,

Taoism, shared consciousness, "Oneness" all human attempts at labeling for what can't be explained, at least in the English language. It is a "Knowing" a Divine Truth that has to be experienced. For me, bumbling through trying to figure out how to make quantum shifts in my knowing, by myself, became a dangerously precarious waterfall of epic proportions.

There are some who have opened and embraced their knowing of the collective consciousness of experience. They have the same gifts we all have, intuition, the "sight", being able to connect with clarity to our very essence, which some call our soul. They have shown up in this time and place to be guides to those of us seeking on the path. It would be easy to mystify the abilities of those who have chosen to share them but the simple truth is that we all have the ability to see.

My Seer is one of these people. She is experienced and studied in transcendent communication or, opening the doorway to clear communication for that which already resides in each one of us. She would show me the door. It was up to me to find the key to unlock it.

I had been working with my Seer for about six months before the window to my soul opened to me for the very first time. We had worked on my attachment issues as I was learning to let go of the ranch property I had just sold. For most of our early sessions we stayed in the present time or ventured back to childhood to repair damaging ideas that had been rooted there. When the ranch finally sold I thought our work was done. I was absolutely wrong.

A few months before Anamchara showed up, I went out with a friend to a yearly town party with a great beer garden and live music. It is a time in our community to see people you normally only see at the grocery store or dropping the kids off at school. I am a very private person, not prone to big barbeques or parties or any type of casual social get-togethers. I don't think that people who see me would see the legacy of painful social shyness that started somewhere in my early 20's. I don't do small talk, the simple conversations that start between strangers that can end up turning into life-long friendship. For me friendship was hard-won and not often pursued. I have always envied people who have the easy way about them that draws people in to start that walk down the road to human intimacy. Social isolation for me was a way of life that had started unconsciously, borne of broken hearts, failed friendships and a disdain for the ordinary bullshit of life. My preference, or choice being a better word at the time, was to be alone with my children. I guess it was safer than saying yes to what life had to offer. My Wicked Ego Witch was always in the background urging me to stay alone because if anyone knew the truth, the lies, the fraud I was, my secret would be revealed for the world to see. I wish I could say what that really meant, since on an intellectual level I know no reasons that I am a fraud, a liar or anything other than a genuine, honest soul with a generous streak the size of Texas. Would the witch EVER look in the mirror and see my truth?

The night was balmy, the music was loud and because of the emotional roller coaster of the ranch sale I started drinking, early and hard. I had a great time, danced with a "kid" half my age and ended up walking home. I don't remember feeling drunk. I charged up the computer, typed a coherent email and went upstairs to bed.

And the terror started. My mind became a monster of the worst kind of nightmare. I couldn't control my thoughts. I got dizzy and sick while the fear overtook me in a form of panic I had never experienced before. I don't know what happens to people who, in a classic sense, lose it. In the back of my mind I always had a paralyzing, irrational fear that I was going to go crazy.

I flew out of my bed, panicked and terror stricken and clung to my angel St Bernard. I curled up into a fetal position on the floor and prayed to every deity I could think of to help me stop the insanity of thoughts tumbling through my mind. The nightmare of thoughts, and I have to admit I don't remember their context today, at the time, seemed unbearable and otherworldly. They weren't thoughts that I had ever thought before aside from the feeling of going crazy. Eventually the panic subsided, I got up, vomited in the toilet and curled up next to my son in bed and fell asleep.

I knew it was time to call my Seer again. I needed some wisdom, the kind of wisdom available to me that comes from my own spiritual self. This is the sight the Seer possesses. Immediately after taking with my seer I wrote this essay, one I had put away completely until my relationship started with the Anamchara man who would be another step on my journey to my own Divine Truth. This is what she had to say after the Ranch sold and my overwhelming feelings of going crazy became too strong to ignore.

The Gift – 7/30/08 - I pulled up alongside a curb in front of a church, just down the street from the hospital, stopped the car and checked the time, a minute before I could make the call. I fidgeted around, and dialed the number. As always, I am met with the breezy air and quiet comfort of the voice on the other end of the line. A voice I've never met before, no face to associate with the name.

The urge to call my Seer again comes during a period of a great emotional tsunami. It felt like clearing away, a letting go, a fury that couldn't be contained. A period of transition, of impending insanity, a release to a new level of spiritual awareness that is just plain stuck. The thought was very clear – call the Seer and call my life coach, who guided me to the Seer if by supreme right order so many months ago.

My life felt constricted, like an over sealed bag stuffed to its point of explosion. The explosion was just on the ho-

rizon, I could feel it. – The feeling, weighted under the unknown or perhaps it was always known just not acknowledged? In retrospect, I doubt it.

I had just narrowly avoided foreclosure of my dream – and when I say narrowly let me define that by saying a matter of hours. The Seer had been helping me at random intervals connect to the power of the property that held me captive so I could release it and let it go. It had been almost a year. This property raging in my psyche and the powerlessness I felt to save it. – That is an entirely different story although connected to this story in a profound and powerful way.

As the property closed and was handed over to its new owner, I was caught off guard to feel a wave of – actually, I don't know what a wave of and that was part of the problem. The feeling was dark and despairing. My sense of self and purpose was gone with the signature on the line releasing the title of the ranch to another. I had expected to feel a wave of relief which never came.

The phone call to the Seer was to help un-earth the feelings in me which I for so long had forgotten or had frankly been too scared to feel. We started the call with the prayer to the Divine and asked that what was about to unfold be given with wisdom, grace and ease – this is how every session starts.

As usual, I was asked what I wanted to talk about and today, I just wanted to see what the Universe could see through me, in the Seer's eyes. Sorrow. She saw transition, transcendence and great sorrow. There is was. The word for what I had been feeling and couldn't describe – great sorrow. Grieving. For the loss of a dream, a part of myself. The words resonated so deeply I could feel the cells in my body start to release. It was a definition, and I do well when things are defined.

I said something about needing to further explore why I was so stuck with emotions, why I was having so much trouble feeling anything. The Seer began the psychic work *backwards and asked me to think of a time when I saw or felt that emotion was dangerous or scary. And honestly, I couldn't do it – I couldn't linearly progress back through my 40 years and say "Ah-ha, this is it.. this is what I saw or thought or did..." But I could see (or feel) that the root of the issue was with my birthmother and the trauma of her relinquishment of me so many years. We talked very briefly about the birthmother, family of origin and she said "Yes, I saw this in your family of origin" And then, she spoke the words "I'm afraid I am going crazy" and then "I'll die." Every cell in my entire body roused at full attention. She spoke the words that have haunted me for years – that I was going to go crazy. Where did that come from I wonder – the basic terror of the feeling of going insane? – That was it.*

With every ounce of me on full hyper alert she spoke the words and the terror became very, very real. She flashed back to a past life and said, "Sometime around 1930's on the East coast, a wealthy family, a husband you went hysterical, they called you crazy and ended up in a mental institution and were given shock therapy – your soul separated entirely from your body." – And she shuddered, it was very clear she saw the vision which thankfully, the Universe spared from me. I knew with every fiber of my being what she said was true – I could feel the terror. My skin was alive with hyper awareness and I literally began to dissociate. And I also knew, this is where this irrational thought came from.

We moved on to another topic but my mind was completely bent. – I couldn't focus on what The Seer was saying and at some point I had to ask her to go back – I needed some closure, some release from this newly acquired consciousness of something so terrifying. For several long moments in time, I was stuck there. We did go back to this place because I needed to process, to think through to make some sense of this. I can't remember the exact words of the conversation but at some point along the way, MY spirit with very clear intent said loudly You will NEVER go there again." And the fear, literally disappeared.

I also had another revelation – that she wasn't crazy at all. – I knew with every fiber of my being that she had been controlled and repressed which probably caused her hysteria but she wasn't crazy. In fact, what I saw very, very clearly was a woman who was full of life as I said to the Seer "She was a cool chick". – And then I saw the repression in myself. Although in this time and space, the repression has been of my own making. I have been so terrified to feel anything for so long. I honestly can't say why.

And then the gift happened. I felt a coming together of the Universe. In support, in harmony and Divine right grace. It was a space of All-Knowing, it was a space of generosity. It was the space where the spirit lives in its full glory. The Seer asked me to breathe into this space and be there. It was an experience without explanation or rationalization. It just was. And in full circle the realization was very, very clear. The feeling of peace so profound it lacks proper explanation.

The reading went on a while longer and many things were discussed about other lifetimes that contained great joy – these were far easier to hear about and remember on a gut level. I felt a space as expansive as the Universe open up to greet me, to meet me on a plane of good, honest true intention because that is who and what I am today as a spirit – good and honest and pure of intention. It is a safe space and one I walk into today without fear.

As the Universe would have it, I also had an appointment with my life coach who guided me to the Seer about 1.5 hours later. Me, being generally a very mentally focused person needed to think and process and make this new sense "make sense". It all became so clear – the patterns, the thoughts about "wealthy men" about "being in total control of my life" – of being afraid of going crazy. All the things I thought about on a rational, intellect based space. It just made so much sense now, the things I can release, the truth of who I am as a spirit.

As the day winds to a close I am opened up fully to "The Gift" – the one handed so gracefully to me by my spirit today. It says, "Suffer no more. Fear no more. Be open to the possibilities of the Divine and welcome the gifts given to you each minute of each day. Be present in the possibility." It says "I am whole and perfect."

I felt such clarity when the session ended. I felt lighter and freer than I had in probably my whole life. What I wasn't prepared for was the aftermath of the sight. It's a difficult thing to balance being human and knowing that more exists in other Universal planes. There is an adjustment that has to be made between the spirit personality and the body personality, the one that encompasses the mind and the ego, the part of each of us that has to feel in control of our own circumstances and destiny. This was my first experience in transcending time and space. My spirit felt free. My ego and control mechanisms were reeling. I felt stuck between two places of knowing and very disconcerted.

Having just been shaken to the center of my own truth, while extremely comforting on one level – left me raw and vulnerable. Knowing something completely and viscerally and having that new truth be integrated into forty years of paradigm doesn't happen easily or without effort. Or, maybe it does, but that just isn't my way. Always struggling for control I have this insatiable need to have to have everything make perfect sense so it can be filed away in a neat little box, only to be taken down from the shelf when chosen. I couldn't make this experience "make sense." I had never had the experience of knowing something so profoundly and having it feel so complete, real and tangible but having it be so otherworldly that words literally haven't been invented to describe the experience.

This is the knowledge that the Seer imparts. As my conversations with the Seer continued to expand over time, so did my knowing and Truth of my own journey. After being shaken to the core with my own past life Truth, it would become more and more challenging to call upon the Seer for her guidance. Once I opened to the consciousness, however scary and intimidating the knowledge, I began to see my life and circumstances in a different way. I began to seek the life experience of expanded consciousness.

Expanded consciousness is the experience of stepping outside, for just a brief moment of being human to see the vastness that exists all around every one of us on this planet today. It's an act of such faith and courage that it defies any logic. The ego centered body personality just doesn't get it. It struggles and fights and the Wicked Ego Witch simply howls in fury to be exposed for her truth, that everything she's ever made you believe is false. It's all lies.

That simply is the truth. It's all lies. Everything I'd ever believed about myself was not true. Great, so, it was all lies? What now? That middle space of leaving the old behind and stepping into something new was utterly confounding, infuriating and fraught with every scheme in the book to get me to return to the comfort of the small space I had just left behind. The Witch screamed louder, it seemed the people in my life stop making any sense. I was left with what felt like nothing. I couldn't go back to being who I used to be but there were no instructions for moving forward into being something new.

At least, given how I viewed the world that's how it felt. I wanted things to be black and white. "Ok, I know too much to be this anymore so I'll close that door and be this over here for awhile." The problem is, the journey is just not that straightforward. There are no black and whites. The journey is simply to stay open, and trusting and be available when the next lesson for more expansion knocks on the door. Sometimes it takes a while for the next lesson to show up. That is the work of Effortless Grace. The space of breath and expansion and simple grace to spend some time resting and reflecting, putting things into perspective so that I would have more tools available when it was time to move forward again. Radical Faith raised her sword and gave me the courage to step back into my lifeboat on the River of life and follow the current to the next life lesson.

The Crossroads…

During dinner with Anamchara I summoned up the courage to ask what I considered to be a delicate question, but one that after all the hours of conversation we shared, had never been asked. I asked him how he came to have lost function on the entire left side of his body. I could see the shadow creep up around the edges of his eyes as he answered me in a clearly rehearsed and often requested answer, "As a child I lived on a huge working cattle ranch. One day I was out riding my horse alone and we got caught in a desert lightening storm. We came galloping down a river valley to where there was a fork just narrow enough to cross. In the center of the river bed, ground strike lightening hit me directly. The impact of the lightening caused me to have a stroke and killed my horse instantly. I was clinically dead several times, according to the people around me and the story I was told when I regained consciousness. My horse absorbed most of the electrical current, died instantly and saved my life."

Anamchara and his life journey had been forever changed by electricity. The moment the sentence came out of his mouth the breath inside my lungs became so dense it was hard to find the strength to exhale. I could feel every cell of my body react to a distant memory locked inside me. The empathy poured out from every pore as I softened my gaze in understanding. At some point on my soul journey I had been forever changed as a result of electricity. The coincidence, even in the moment could not be overlooked.

The first evening with him ended outside, at our cars and far too early at my choice. Suddenly and without warning I had this unquenchable desire to run, to get away – as far and as fast as I could from this man. He was nothing but delightful company and hadn't treated me in any way that should have evoked such a reaction, but I just had to go. He leaned in to kiss me just as a group of young and handsome men passed by. I hesitated, partially from embarrassment I think or perhaps not, perhaps in retrospect it was fear. I kissed him back but felt nothing, no chemistry, no spark and I panicked, said goodbye and left, as fast as I could.

The truth is, and one I fully and completely admit not only to myself but to him as well is that I honestly have no idea why our relationship didn't end in that moment. There should have been no more to our story together. But, it didn't end there, because it never got started and to have walked away then would have been to say no to the journey, to the possibility. We talked over the next several days on the phone and went right back to the same intense level of intellectual and spiritual connection we could always find in our conversations. And then he asked again, would I be willing to meet him for another dinner?

To this day I still have absolutely no idea why I said yes, no idea whatsoever. When I saw him again for the second time, the intensity changed. We found in that first moment a depth of connection that still today defies explanation. In that moment, we simply stared into each other's eyes with a connection that went straight to the center of my soul, a living déjà vu. We had been here before. It was a knowing, as though through our eyes we could see something so much deeper and connected than feels possible on a normal human level. In the beginning, this moment used to scare me. I would feel fear.

I wonder about instinct and intuition. In that moment in time, when what I was feeling was fear, why didn't I just stop and walk away? What happens at the crossroads when we make the decision to move through fear instead of honor it and walk away? How do we really know when fear is our intuition protecting us from something just ahead? In these early days, the fear inside of me would be met with an equal courage to keep going forward. Perhaps it was the start of the Wicked Ego Witch and Radical Faith doing their first baby steps of the dance for control.

In the first moments of being in the same physical space as my Anamchara, that's what I'd feel. Equal parts fear and courage. It's hard to say why Radical Faith won out, I was still too unconscious to know there was a dance between fear and courage going on, but, Faith always won out and I'd find myself staring into his eyes again. On this second night, the moment of fear shifted quickly and quietly into perfect grace and ease, and we moved into a new place of physical connection and comfort. As we walked through the restaurant we were seated in a quiet corner with windows to the trendy street on one side and a roaring fireplace on the other. Dinner again, was spectacular but tonight the conversation was so robust and connected that I forgot we were surrounded by a sea of people eating around us. Our conversation flowed smoothly and effortlessly shifted from one topic to another. As our meal ended, Anamchara had another surprise. I'd never been to this restaurant nor in actuality even knew it existed, which was kind of a surprise since I loved this particular area of town. As the waitress cleared our dinner dishes, she handed us the desert menu.

When she returned, our entire table was filled with every kind of dessert imaginable. Anamchara and I, forks in hand, together jumped head-first into the sugary sweetness of the divine confection spread out before us. I fed him, he fed me, we laughed and talked and in that moment in time I felt something shift. Something fell into place.

We left the restaurant to walk around and began to window shop. We walked as lovers, my arm gently draped over his. We talked robustly as we walked and gazed with longing at some art pieces carefully appointed in the shop windows around us. At one point, I was goofing around acting silly and turned straight into a picture window with my face. I actually left a lipstick print on the window. We roared hilariously as it began to rain.

It was starting to get late and time to think about heading home as he walked me to my car, but this time it felt so much different. I wasn't in a hurry to leave. I wanted to linger there, in the place we had found together but it was late and the rain that had started as a gentle mist of persistence turned to a tempestuous torrent of sheets driving down upon us.

As we stood together in that transitional goodbye moment he pulled me into him and kissed me with such a fire that I literally felt the Universe shift on its axis. We melted into each other as I could taste the sweetness of promise and passion. Our lips fit together as if they had been made to only kiss the other. It was the kiss I had waited for my whole life. And we kissed, and kissed and stayed locked together in the pouring rain for what seemed like hours. In a moment of breath, I felt a mysterious pull that bordered somewhere between panic and pure ecstasy. With our eyes locked together I felt a connection so deep and so intense that I felt catapulted to another time and space. I couldn't distinguish where he ended and I began. It was a place I had never been before with another. I looked deep inside his intense gaze and said, "You are not for the faint of heart." He smiled his mischievous smile and answered, "No, I am not." A shiver of goose-flesh spiraled its way up my spine. It was almost a dare. Anamchara threw down his gauntlet as Radical Faith unsheathed her sword.

That should have been enough intensity to freak me out completely and send me running. The level of passion, intensity and genuine knowing of this person, so soon should have been way too much. I could not say no to the Anamchara and his heart song journey. Even if I wanted to, it was too late. We had a soul agreement with each other to keep and the journey was just beginning.

Our conversations continued by phone, always starting late and ending so early that for me, it would soon be another day. I looked forward to my late night phone calls and the stories and connection that would always come. Our talks grew more and more passionate. There were times when I could feel his presence of intensity, sexuality and passion right in the room with me. It came time to see what would come next, and true to my own nature made the first move and proposed a weekend together.

As the weekend drew closer, I began to be filled with fear so huge, and so ominous that I could sense the dragons peering ominously from their caves waiting to engulf me in their fires of terror. The closer the weekend got, the more afraid I became. I don't know when I became so full of fear. I used to be fearless as a child, and probably long into my early adulthood. Maybe I became afraid after I became a mother, who knows? At that moment in time, the fear was paralyzing. I went back and forth a thousand times, with a thousand more excuses to not go to him. I could see the reflection of the blonde spiked madness of the Wicked Ego Witch in the mirror as I waged my internal battle of fear and insecurity. In the next second, the glint of jewels on the scabbard and the heart shaped rubies captured my attention as Radical Faith urged me to move on.

As I've aged I don't like to be away from my own space and things familiar. I was getting ready to go to a place I didn't know, to a house in the middle of nowhere with a man who evoked as much terror as passion in me. The fight was visceral, the fear was real. Radical Faith in her resplendent glowing peacefulness was insistent, the musical lilt in her voice growing louder and calmer as she used her gentle musings of Trust and Truth to persuade me to keep walking. Effortless grace whispered quietly, her long shimmery black hair gently blowing the wind; "Believe. The journey has only just begun." Together, they packed my bags and pointed my truck in the direction of what lay ahead.

The Ones that Came Before…

On the yellow brick road of highway before me, I began to think about all the men who had come before the Anamchara in my long and winding history of relationships past. The good, the bad and the ones I simply just had no use for along the way. The ones I used for redemption and worthiness. The ones I used out of loneliness and despair to make the journey a bit more tolerable. There were good ones that I really tried to love but because I was deaf to my own Truth and the wisdom that was contained in the journey, I chose to walk away from in fear, the fear of being exposed, of being seen, and ultimately of being left. The seductive and smoky voice of the Wicked Ego Witch was the only sound I could hear as the men from my past stepped up to guide me, once again, through the lessons of the past.

I started my journey in Heart Space very young. I was always seeking, even from a very early age and as I hit puberty I was seeking through relationship desperately trying to find the partner who would save me and fill the gaping hole inside. I had my heart broken over and over again before I even hit 18. It is such a sad thing to be a broken little girl who believes that sex equals love. "He'll love me and never leave me if I do this or this or that," is such a lie, God my Wicked Ego Witch started early. I was so insecure that I started seeking validation in another person. I started with such a deficit that even if I had been loved in return, I loathed myself so much that I couldn't accept it. That is tragic. It is also worth mentioning that because I was so insecure my choices weren't so stellar either. I can look back today and really see some of the men in my past—some of them so broken, and the more broken they were, the more I loved them and sought validation in their touch. If they loved me, and assuredly some did, I did everything humanly possible to make sure they saw the truth, or at least the Wicked Ego Witch's truth, that I was completely unworthy of love. One way or another, either through really poor choices to begin with or very foolish behaviors, all of my relationships ended.

It isn't to say I didn't marry. I did, fairly young. I married a man for whom I had no feelings of love at all. I just wanted to be married. I guess I figured "being married" would fill the gaping hole that had grown so large that it threatened to envelop me entirely. He was a great guy, one I'd love to run into again to see who he has turned out to be, but there was no emotional or spiritual connection between us at all. We divorced after a couple of years, and the cavernous hole raging inside me started desperately seeking the next man to fill the gap.

And then I found him, my first experience with love at first sight. It was on a dance floor in a country bar and I looked up – straight into the eyes of a sorcerer who wove his spellbinding dark magic around me. We collided together and shared every moment as we became entangled in a love affair overnight. The world revolved around being with this man. My entire existence became completely dependent on the future plans we were making. I could see the whole fantasy picture, the perfect wedding, the gorgeous children, the happily ever after. I was completely 110% sure I had found the one man who could and would fill the cavernous space growing inside me. For a brief moment in time, the hole seemed to close up. I was content, I was euphoric and I was in love. But, the parts of me still so broken, so disconnected from my truth started the dance of the private internal torture of self-doubt. The Wicked Witch started her howling.

And then came his truth. His dark side and fragile shell of stage props and false innuendo quickly turned into my nightmare. He cheated, he lied. He tried to strangle me in a parking lot. He came home drunk and locked me in the bedroom with his shotgun pointed at the door. It was all confirmed. I was a horrible, unlovable person and he was going to leave me. I clung to him, desperate. I prayed, I starved myself, I forgave his transgressions and I begged him for another chance. Whatever happened must have been my fault. He must have seen my truth and was treating me the way I must have deserved to be treated. It never occurred to me that he was the one damaged and broken. It never crossed my mind that no human being who is even remotely stable and in control tries to strangle another or hold her hostage at gunpoint. No the Witch was too loud in my head singing her sultry lies, "You are getting exactly what you deserve."

We got pregnant. I am pretty sure that I know exactly when that happened. In a bout of "God, I'm so sorry, I can't believe I cheated and lied, please forgive me," sex. And I did. I forgive him until about a week later, when I came home to our apartment we had so lovingly decorated together and found the electricity, phone and cable shut off and the furniture gone. I was pregnant with his child, and he had just walked out. Wow. The Wicked Ego Witch was right again. I went back to begging and pleading, desperately trying to engage him to be a part of our lives, all the while knowing he had left me to move in with another. It didn't take but a nod in confirmation from the Witch, and I was certain. I was so unlovable, that even pregnant, I didn't deserve to be loved. I miscarried our child at 14 weeks. He never called to say I'm sorry; he never did anything at all. Still, I held on, for several more months praying he'd come to his senses and come back to me. He didn't, thank God.

That was my first glimpse at Effortless Grace, though I had no idea of her beauty and truth at the time. She had given me a moment of true Grace, but I was so lost and broken, I wasn't even conscious of the higher truth stepping in to save me from a fate far worse than what I'd been through. I was saved. I was just too broken and unconscious to know anything other than I got what I deserved. The waterfall of self-hatred and destruction had only just begun.

After this relationship ended I was broken, so completely broken that I looked to every external mechanism to "fix myself" that I could find. I was so disconnected from my Truth and absolutely hypnotized by the ranting of the Witch it never even occurred to me the work I needed to do should have started from the inside. I committed myself 100% to perfection. I was never going to find myself again in a place where I wasn't physically good enough for a man. Wow, what a detour. I exercised like a fiend, I starved myself and I woke up one morning in a damn near perfect little body with an attitude to match. No one was ever going to make me feel unworthy again. I didn't need anyone to make me feel unworthy the Witch made sure it was crystal clear, I was unworthy.

I packed my bags and left that state in a matter of one month and one trip. I couldn't run away fast enough from the man who held me with such dark magic. I was all alone starting my new life, and I could create myself to be anyone or anything I wanted to be. For the first time in my life, I was physically beautiful. I guess I am either fortunate or not, depending on your perspective, to have grown into my physical self. I was not an attractive child and stayed chunky and clunky until my 20's. My relationships were built on my personality and my neediness. I had no road map to guide me on the path of an entire new paradigm. In this new world I really could just smile and look pretty and "be enough," enough for what and for whom? I lost all sense of who I was and what I stood for.

It was a long, lonely and dark journey in this stretch of the River and I coped the only way I knew how.

It was a major adjustment to my psyche to be "seen" by men as physically desirable. I built a wall of aloof bitchiness around me. I called it, "If you aren't strong enough to get past the wall, you aren't strong enough period." I guess I thought the right man would be strong enough to break through my defenses and prove himself to be the one who wouldn't ever leave me. When you're broken, all you attract is broken in return and when you attract broken, they simply just aren't in a position to help you at all. It really didn't matter the how high the wall was that I built, the next life lesson was about to show up. Sometimes things need to be completely destroyed to be rebuilt. I guess I needed more destruction. The Wicked Ego Witch was firmly at the helm of my lifeboat in the River with Niagara Falls just ahead.

I remember getting ready to go out one night, seeking the next conquest, or victim, depending on your perspective, and my best friend looked me dead in the eye. She said one sentence that likely had more impact on me than any other sentence anyone has ever spoken to me out loud. She said, "You are so beautiful on the inside. What happened to her?" While even in the moment, the sentence had impact, the Wicked Ego Witch puffed up to scream and yell her rants of inadequacy. In retrospect it is a surprise that I heard my best friend at all, and that her words cracked the surface of my armor. Her words were the first whispers of the battle cry of Radical Faith, that change was ahead and possible, if only I'd be brave enough to follow it. Unfortunately, I was still too broken, and bravery was a long time away.

Wildly passionate and unpredictable are the only words to describe the next Heart Song journey. We were fire and ice, two fractions of a very broken circle that consumed each other in every way. We were well matched intellectually, and that just made the games simply far more cruel. Our bodies melded together as if at the heights of our passion we might find healing from the gushing arterial wounds our previous relationships had left behind. We couldn't fill the gaping holes inside each other as much as we tried.

For as much destruction as the previous relationship had wreaked on my physical self, this one called out all the old destructive emotional stuff. I believe that we both really tried to love the other but we were too very broken souls, completely disconnected from our own Divine truth to find any common stable ground to build a foundation upon. We tried, and in trying we pulled out and played every dirty rotten relationship trick that can be played. More often than not, alcohol was present, more in me than in him. The alcohol gave me the false courage to be scathing and raw with all the built up scarred emotion of ugliness I carried inside of me. Believe me when I say there was a river of self-hatred, lost hopes and dreams to flood any possibility of having any real intimate connection with another. And the flood came – often in manic outbursts and public screaming matches under the neon lights and pulsating music of our stage. Our relationship was very public. We were kind of pseudo-celebrities in our small little world. My humiliation was very public, my emotional instability got thrown wide open for the world to see. I was so broken that I honestly didn't care what people saw or what they thought. I allowed myself to act in ways that today, still make me cringe and are too painful to write. Our relationship finally came to the place where we both had to, at least at surface value, let go. By now, between the two back to back relationships—any heart I had left was gone.

In a flight of fancy I met another man, an easy man. We had a lot of fun together and my life became more than spending my evenings dancing in a country bar. He took me to beautiful places and showed me what it means to be alone and connected in nature. It was an amazing gift. Eventually we moved in together out of convenience and a few weeks later, I became pregnant. I miscarried this pregnancy the day after I learned it existed. I remember clearly standing in our bedroom doorway as I told him of the miscarriage. "You must be really happy," I said. He looked at me with such compassion and grace and simply said, "Children are a blessing." And then he said we might want to think about being more careful. Two weeks later I was pregnant again. I will always believe this man came into my life for one purpose, to give me the gift of my son. Our relationship ended at the 12 week pregnancy mark. He left without much fanfare and I was pregnant and alone, again.

It was at this crossroads I decided that I was never going to love again. I was going to lock away my heart because it was far too painful, the ending always written on the wall from the beginning. I would dedicate my life to raising my son, and building stability that to this point had been completely elusive in my life. The price I paid for that choice came in bitterness and regret. And it worked, for years.

My biological legacy is one of impressive intelligence and ruthless female strength. Men were simply a necessary distraction but weren't needed for any long term purpose. It was written in our family female genetic code. It's interesting to me the whole nature vs. nurture debate – in every regard, but in this regard specifically, the apple didn't fall far from the tree. I was adopted as an infant. I was given to others to raise, by my then 17 year old birthmother who had no choice in the decision to hand her child to strangers, the day after I was born. In my life, my adoptive parents stayed married until I was in my early 20's. My father was a very important person in my life, so highly intelligent and well educated you would have thought my choices in partners would have followed suit. No, I always traveled down the food chain, not up. Perhaps it was the control factor again, in fact, I am sure it was. I was never comfortable with a man who rivaled me in any way in intelligence and I damn sure wasn't comfortable with a man who had any money at all.

When I finally put the Seer's story of my past lifetime in context with the legacy of relationships I had chosen, it became crystal clear to me why a man who I felt had any intellectual or financial foothold on me was completely terrifying. In this past lifetime, a man with standing and money had a part of my soul committed, and eventually electro-shocked into a soul shattering fugue. According to the Seer, this woman, in this lifetime, died shortly thereafter. The Seer has said to me several times that our bodies hold energy patterns of past lifetimes, that situations can trigger energetic reactions and patterns in us that don't make any sense based on current circumstances or present life history. The minute I was made conscious of this repeating pattern, the stranglehold broke, at least I thought so. I felt like I was waking up from being completely unconscious and it was only the beginning of the Heart Song journey.

Hayden Ranch...

As thoughts of relationship past left me, and the road got closer and closer to Anamchara, the dance between the Wicked Ego Witch and Radical Faith raged. The terror I had felt began to shift and morph into Effortless Grace. I had conquered my fear and taken the next step on the journey to go to him. My mind wheeled and spun around as if pieces of a puzzle where showing up to guide me to some insight that would be important along the way. A familiar longing edged up along my spine, and as it peeked into my consciousness, another piece of the puzzle dropped into view.

Part of my initial attraction to Anamchara was a feeling I just couldn't shake that we were meant to do some sort of work together. Our basic internal drive and life work was too similar in its nature, our journey in this regard seemed to be parallel. I was incredibly attracted to the vision and passion that he carried. When he spoke of his work, I could feel the power and truth of what it means to be standing fully in one's own power to create the life of their choosing. The connection between his life work and my hopes and dreams for the future couldn't be overlooked and carried with it the possibility of a full life partnership in every way. Anamchara had a lifelong dream of creating a land space where humans and animals could partner together to do spiritually healing work. Purchasing his large acreage property was a step, in a long line of many steps he had taken to make this vision a reality. Specifically, Anamchara worked with horses. In his work, horses partner with people, particularly youth working on issues around trust, fear and connection. He does this in the tradition of Native American sacred hoop teachings. This connection seemed magical to me given the fact that we had such similarities, like my passion and natural draw to horses and also my background in social services. Part of me believed there must be a place for me on this sacred land. Maybe his land could replace the land I had just lost?

Winding my way through the juniper tree-lined back country, high desert roads that led to his home, I felt a mixture of pure panic and addictive adrenaline. As the roads twisted and turned my thoughts bounced wickedly between turning around and going home, and stepping down harder on the gas pedal to reach him faster. The trees parted as I neared his long gravel driveway. Anamchara had told me early on that his property was still in the building stages. He was trying desperately to find the funding to further his mission, part of that was finding the way to build permanent structures on the land. I slowed to a crawl in my truck as the disrepair of the driveway became a four-wheel navigation around enormous pot holes. Where would I find myself? Signs of human life were absent as I picked my way cautiously closer to where he was waiting. Around the next bend in the road stood the most incredible sheer black horse I had ever seen. So black that she appeared blue as the sun cascaded across her mane and shone iridescently across her taut lean body. Her eyes danced wildly as if she'd been waiting for my arrival. She whinnied, as if to say "The time has come," and galloped away through the rolling desert cactus and sage to find comfort and safety in her waiting herd just beyond the distant horizon.

I made my way back to the barn and found a dirt road leading off into the distance. My directions said I could park at the barn or drive all the way back up to the homestead. I chose to keep driving as the denseness of the desert juniper trees surrounded me once again. Just ahead in the distance was a very small wooden building with a faint trickle of smoke dancing off the roof-line. The ramshackle structure had seen better days, the porch dangled precariously as if to shout warning of caution and safety to those entering the threshold of his home. To my surprise I felt warmth and love despite the primitive conditions. Grandmother evergreens surrounded this place if by some mysterious and magical presence. How had a dense grove of evergreens taken root in this place? Because I was starting to pay attention I could hear them whisper their welcome of peace and love. A surprising desert oasis stream babbled its message of time, truth and trust as it danced beside me and continued its journey under a small bridge that would take me directly to his door.

When I finally glanced toward the front door, I found him in a beautiful birch chair lightly napping in the warmth of the surprise sun in early winter. He was wrapped in an alpaca rug with his feet gently propped on a hand-carved tree trunk table. I could stop there, in that moment with the Anamchara quietly napping and see his innocence, his compassion and the love that he radiated, even in his sleep. I could feel the magic contained in this land. It was the same connection I had found with my own. The memories flooded back...

May 2005 – Leaving the title company I had just done the impossible. I had just signed twenty pages of loan documents to close and own my very first home. Never doing things half-way, I had signed on the dotted line to own a 32 acre estate costing more than I probably had earned total in my entire lifetime. The first time I saw the Ranch is etched in my mind with a clarity and magnitude of detail. It was like the loving eyes of a mother seeing her child for the very first time. It was like memorizing every detail of a child's gorgeous pink skin, the wrinkles in their fingers and toes and how a mother can memorize the slightest nuance of their cry. It is that level of excruciatingly beautiful detail that I remember.

Soaring vaults of enormous beams traversed the ceiling in the great room, the fireplace so grand, so encompassing was built entirely of river-rock and large enough so that I could stand in its open center. I could almost feel the heat of the roaring winter fires to come. The craftsmanship at the Ranch was exquisite. The feel of this home was distinctly old world. It had incredible stained glass windows with leaded accents in hidden spots and an old barn wood floor that had the character and charm of all those who had walked it before me. I could feel the love here. It radiated from the center of the earth, the peace, the love, the hopes and dreams that had been built here. Until my last breath I will always be certain about the magic contained in the land of my Ranch. It is a place of such transcendent beauty and healing that just the thought of the long walks I had winding through the trees can take me to a place of profound peace and simple knowing of the truth of the Universe and its mysteries. I knew I had a journey to take here. Maybe it was that center, the balance – the feel, that made this property "my one," one of the many detours on the journey that would have profound lessons to teach me if I'd only stop long enough to breathe and reflect. Some lessons are meant to happen. Some things are just simply destiny. At face value, there was no way in the world I could afford the price tag attached to my dream. The Universe had provided me with a playground of learning opportunities, the opportunity to see myself and where I had been, who I had become and challenged me to stay present and open to whatever might come.

Within 15 minutes of walking into the grand open space of the great room, my fate was sealed. I would walk any distance and face any obstacle to come to this place. This was my dream, my chance to have everything I had ever wanted, my first home, a place to have my animals and my children. It was every fantasy I had ever had. My first idea was to approach the owner to see if he would be willing to carry a contract because given my financial situation, was there was no way a bank was going to finance me on a property of this magnitude, both in terms of sales price, and of acreage. I didn't have the documentable income to even come within a fraction of what should have been necessary. So, in my true undeniable business fashion, I prepared a proposal and sat down in the very center of the great room of this house and opened the doors to possibility.

My first meeting with the owner of the property is one I will forever remember. He is an amazing human being --compassion, grace and life lessons radiate from the center of his being. He is a kind and generous man and we easily formed a business relationship. In a series of interesting co-incidences, if there is such a thing, I was able to get bank financing for the majority of the property's value. The owner was willing to carry a silent second mortgage without payments which enabled me to meet the bank obligation for the first couple of years. The only additional criteria requested by this negotiation, was that my father had to personally guarantee the second mortgage in case of default. For reasons that still I don't understand, my father was willing to do this for me and signed to be personally responsible if something happened. These were the heydays of easy money, with banks bending over backwards and not checking financial worthiness of its loan customers. I felt it was just destined to be because it was coming together under circumstances that should have never fallen together. When you open the door to possibility, the Universe will always answer. I have heard it said, "Careful what you wish for, you're likely to get it." I got exactly what I wanted and the journey began.

The night I closed the loan I took my son to our new home. With just towels, and not another stick of furniture, all I wanted to do was take a bath in my new claw foot tub. I wanted to wander around and hear the whisperings of the grandmother evergreens with their roots stretching to the center of the earth. I wanted to picture all the animals that I could bring here. This was it, this is what would fill the cavernous hole in the center of my being. I had finally found it. All my hopes and dreams and all my self-worth got tied up in the magic and hope of this enchanted land.

God I learned so much. I learned so much about the truth of my strength, my dedication and my true grit as a sovereign soul on this planet. While I did have help from time to time, managing 32 pristine acres while taking care of the animals that showed up to learn their lessons in this place, as I worked full time to raise my son would become all-consuming. I loved every minute of the solitude of driving the tractor to clear the pasture, clearing branches and downed trees with my truck. I learned absolute self-sufficiency and how not to whine. I learned that, damn, I am strong. I have a tenacious character that didn't give up when the lights went black in a storm or when a tree fell across the driveway and I couldn't get back to the house to my son. I learned how to adapt and overcome when the tractor battery was dead and out of desperation had to drag a chain that weighed at least 75 lbs and was over ten feet long, over a half-mile from the point on the road where I could hook it to my truck and yank that damned tree out of the way. I learned that I didn't need a man around to climb on the roof and unclog the gutters, or split firewood or help me catch the horses and llamas that escaped the pasture fence. I was a warrior woman in my sovereign state all by myself. And the truth was, I liked it.

Now was that really true? Was I really all by myself? No, absolutely not. I had a lot of help, people who came by in the time of need to lend a hand and it was always appreciated. But, the property didn't fill the cavernous hole burning inside me. It didn't build the bridge between the reality of my life and the reality of my soul journey. When I allowed myself a quiet moment, all I felt was empty and alone. I was busy, so it was hard to stop long enough to give that much thought. I thought if I worked harder, brought in more rescue horses or found my next journey the hole so deep and cavernous inside of me would stay closed up, at least for a while longer anyways.

Always the seeker, I kept seeking. I kept seeking because the Wicked Ego Witch kept screaming her shocking, seemingly self-evident truths. "You are not good enough. What makes you think you deserve a million dollar home? You are a fraud! Someone's going to find out that at the end of the day you don't have two pennies to rub together. You are a liar and a cheat and if anyone finds out the truth, you know you'll lose this property. You'll fail, you always do." Evil, horrendous tape loops of near 40 years of prophesy. And I believed her, the Witch. She was always right. I did always lose everything that mattered to me, I knew her high pitched squeals of inadequacy and failure, were true.

My lifelong dream was to own a ranch where I could have horses, where I could watch them and thrive in the peace and joy I can always find when I'm around them. I'd spent a great deal of time working in different organizations that brought horses and people together, mostly around hippo-therapy or partnering with horses to help humans adjust and hopefully overcome physical limitations. One day, while teaching lessons, one of the horses I was working with became spooky about something in his environment. Overconfident and very arrogantly I decided I was going to help him overcome his fear. I jumped on him and marched him right over to the "boogie man" he could sense just outside the arena. Without the balance and security of having my feet in stirrups, because I was too lazy or stupid at the time to be cautious, he spooked and I fell.

The Ranch was my dream, I wanted to have horses around me but I was too terrified to climb back on another one after the fall so I turned to horse rescue. I brought in horses whenever I'd get the call that one was in need. I got them well and found them new forever homes but I could never overcome my fear and climb back on. By doing horse rescue I felt like I was giving back and honoring my deficit based stewardship of this magical land. I was so busy doing, that I stopped listening to the wisdom of the grandmother evergreens whispering their universal truths. I stopped seeing the buds of creation on newly sprouted spring flowers. It was all work, all consuming and I was drowning. At the height of the market I put my Ranch back up for sale, with a price tag high enough to guarantee me the ability to move on gracefully to the next stretch of my life's River. And, I made the decision to adopt my daughter.

Much like with the house, I was drawn to her, the forlorn, sad eyes of an abandoned infant a world away. I was seeking again, following another life journey and circle. I had been adopted as well, as an infant. In truth, I have the fairy tale adoption story. I was well-loved and supported in my precocious early childhood. However controversial my truth about adoption is this: no matter how much I was loved by my adoptive family, the Wicked

Ego Witch screamed throughout my lifetime the one basic truth that I was unloved and unlovable. I was not good enough for the one person, my birth mother, to have kept me. There was something so intrinsic and wrong that I was given away. And for me, another basic truth, everything I loved would go away.

At 34 years old, some years before I bought the Ranch, I was reunited with my biological family. I had never borne any ill will towards the woman who gave me life, understanding through the eyes of a single woman, and single mother myself, that sometimes life hands you situations in which you have no control. I did understand intellectually that the decision to have a baby, and give it to another must be a critical life choice that has lasting emotional consequences. My reunion story was fairy tale. It was the happy ending every adopted child ever wants. Immediately from the first moments I heard my birth mothers voice I knew I was loved, I was never forgotten and my loss was mourned. In fact, I feel very sad to reflect that my birth mother still bears the lasting scars of being forced to give away her baby. She literally kept me in her heart and mourned my loss up until the moment we found each other again. Today, my birth mother is my friend. She is a window to myself to who I might have become if I had not been given the miracle of our reunion. To this day I don't believe she's ever forgiven herself for the circumstances that led her to the outcome of handing her baby to strangers, the baby whose story and outcome she wouldn't know until 34 years later. The sadness and self-hatred remain evident in her choices, her words and her life story. My gift in the reunion, if I were to have chosen to accept it was freedom, freedom from the Wicked Ego Witch and her ranting that tainted every love relationship I had ever tried to engage in. Even knowing that the words of the Witch were wrong – that I was loved, I was not abandoned and that I was worthy of love, the years of hearing her truth were too entrenched into my definition of who and what I was to have its power erased. On this stretch of my River of Life my boat was beached on the rocks of circumstances beyond my control. My sense of identity and view of the world were too defined, my heart too closed. My Ranch was named for my biological family "Hayden Ranch."

For my 35th birthday I was given one of my most treasured gifts. My biological sister, a gifted artist, took the three words and symbolism I had carried throughout my life and wove them into a tattoo. Faith, Hope and Love are the foundational elements I have always carried with me as my motto for trying to navigate my River of Life, at least intellectually. I asked my biological sister to take a cross for hope, an anchor for faith and hearts for love, in a Celtic cross pattern to represent my Irish heritage. She did this beautifully and my biological mother, in my birth town, took me to have my first tattoo. It was another circle of life coming together on the journey. I carry it with me forever as a reminder to silence the Witch and to own my own Truth as it is revealed to me. If only it was that easy to always remember.

When I made the decision to adopt my daughter, the cavernous space inside me started to close up again if for only a brief moment in time. I think I always knew that someday I would adopt. In some sense, it felt a karmic obligation for the blessings that had been bestowed upon me in my own adoption story. I believe that the triad of adoption is so personal, and so filled with its own baggage that it's hard to relate to or understand unless you have lived through it. This was the circle I hoped to draw for my daughter. I want to be the one who understands her and can help her navigate what it means to be different in this world, to help her face and understand the inherent challenges that being adopted can bring. I hope that as this part of my River of Life, and hers unfolds, the reasons we were brought together will become clear and the lessons and healing will be profound for both of us.

That story is still being written.

When I made the decision to move ahead with the adoption I was certain that my Ranch would sell making the thousands of dollars for international adoption possible. I will forever be humbled and grateful to my family who believed in me, more than I believed in myself, that stepped forward financially to make her adoption possible as the days stretched into a year of the property going unsold.

Holding on to the faith necessary to believe that I actually would be able to bring my daughter home and trusting that it would all work out was my very first conscious glimmer of Radical Faith and Effortless Grace. They don't shout, they whisper. They are the kind and compassionate ones that speak of Divine Truth and connection to all that is real and good. They are quiet and speak in whispers of the soul that are so easy to overlook because of their very nature. Radical Faith carries the sword of Truth and Trust and her beautiful sister, Effortless Grace carries her shield of Protection and Peace. I gave my intention clearly to the Universe and moved out of the way with faith and trusted what needed to come together to make it happen would find its way.

The day finally came, my daughter's second birthday, when we got word that we had received travel approval from China to bring her home. I was already a single mother to the most incredible son, I worked full time, I owned 32 acres of paradise with enough animals to take care of to keep someone working from home full time, and I was packing my bags to bring home my two year old daughter who had spent her entire life in an orphanage. My Ranch, still hadn't sold.

I would absolutely never, ever change my decision to adopt my daughter. That is a step on the journey I am still living. It does not escape me, however, how I had overloaded my life so completely that even if the wisdom of the grandmother evergreens that surrounded me on my Ranch, turned to deafening screams, I would not have had the energy or the time to hear them.

When we returned home with my daughter, things went downhill financially at warp speed. I had been living penny to penny just to keep the mortgage paid, and within months, my adjustable mortgage escalated and my second mortgage balloon came due. I watched my life, and my dreams begin to fall apart. I tried harder and harder to maintain control. The harder I held on to unrealistic hopes and dreams at the start of the worst mortgage crisis in US history, the more damage was done. I was the mother and sole support to two beautiful children who needed me. I was so lost I had nothing to give. They had no clue I knew how to laugh or have fun. This is probably the perspective of the Witch, but it is what I believed. I was truly walking dead and in perpetual wait, waiting, endless days of waiting for the right family to show up to buy my house at a price that would enable me to move on. I went from the possibility of making a six figure profit, to barely making enough to pay fees and then the bottom dropped out. My interest rate on a jumbo loan went from 7 to over 12%. The second mortgage came due. I tried to negotiate with the bank and they said "Sorry, you don't make enough money for us to keep your payments at the level where you were meeting your payment – we can't consider restructuring unless you are missing payments." SERIOUSLY? I mean… oh never mind. The history of what happened with the backwards negotiation of the banking industry is now self-evident. I was just one of the first. If I missed one payment, given the huge amount of the monthly payment, my credit would be ruined. This was a huge issue for me but, I had no choice. The grandmother evergreens started whispering more and more loudly… "Let it go.." I had no choice but to give up my sovereign control and let it all fall.

And it fell, and as it fell the Wicked Ego Witch howled in delight at being right again. She was very clear,

I was not deserving I was a failure. Not only had I made a choice to get so far in over my head in this property, but, I had my fathers financial future tied up right along with mine. He had signed a promissory note that guaranteed if I defaulted on the second mortgage, he would be responsible. This was a healthy six figure debt and it wasn't an amount of money that a check could cover. Not only had I failed myself, my children, and my animals—I had failed my father and in doing so, would not only destroy myself, but him as well. I let my dream, my hope and my future slip into the road of foreclosure.

In the meantime, the man who was holding my second mortgage started contacting me to see what my plans were to pay off the second. What eventually happened over the course of the foreclosure journey is nothing short of Divine grace. This man was so amazing that he stayed with me, patient throughout the entire journey – giving me ideas, giving me time and giving me hope that my father wouldn't be ruined right along with me.

It was at this place on my journey that I was led to first contact my Seer. I was in a place of absolute desperation and hoped that someone, something, quite frankly anything could help me figure out how to end this cycle with the Ranch. The morning I made my very first phone call to the Seer I was blessed with a beautiful early summer morning. Sitting outside, surrounded by the beauty and majesty of old growth evergreens we started our session with a prayer for the highest and best good of information to come through.

At some point in the conversation, the Seer called to the "lady of the land" in her words, *"A powerful Diva who watches over this sacred space."* The moment she spoke the words, the sun came through the top of the evergreens and I could see this ethereal being. A clear peace surrounded me as the Seer spoke. *"The Diva honors your stewardship of this land. The land always takes care of it self, it has a journey, a destiny all of its own. She appre-*

ciates your attachment and worry that you have failed, somehow let the land down. You have not. Let it go. The land has agreements with others who will find their way here." In a moment it was like the weight of failure had been removed. I guess that was my biggest fear – that the property would foreclose and I would have been the failure that caused it.

A good portion of my early conversations with my Seer were about my direct past, of my feeling of inadequacy and seeking out those young parts of me, the child in me who had wounds yet to heal. One of the most interesting aspects to me about working with my Seer is that she never makes predictions. She has always been clear that we have free will. We do have "possibility agreements," and different scenarios "mocked up" for our next growth period but, that the future of any soul is subject to the choices we make. I have always found that strangely comforting. I like that I do get the choice, that there is always a crossroads where I can choose to go right or left. Being human, I like choice, even though I continued to walk in a journey where I felt I had none. One of the "possibility agreements" she saw was a family who might come to the property to raise children – foster children or something close. I was quieted in my endless waiting for a moment in time. Something about this property always called to it people or animals that needed to heal. I had always pictured this land being used for a higher purpose. That one of the possibilities might be that foster children could run free in this sacred space, felt very right.

I wish life was as simple as to say "Ah ha, I finally got it, now I get what I want and can move on," but it isn't always that clear nor that easy. Often lessons continue just when you think you've learned them all. While the Ranch and I remained stuck in the process of life lessons and learning to let go, the next steward of this magical land did not show up, and the foreclosure clock kept ticking.

One day, after endless disappointments, failed showings and nonsensical telephone calls to the bank, I just lost it. Part of my trouble with walking dead through my life was that I had literally stopped having any emotional reaction to anything at all. Being a fairly vocal and volatile child, and even more so as a neurotic young woman it came as a welcome respite to feel nothing, I couldn't get hurt that way. Nothing really ever touched that center of emotional truth for me. Something that day triggered a long lost river of emotion in me. During a conversation with my mother I fell to my knees in guilt and shame for losing the one thing I thought mattered most to my future. I was crushing myself under the weight of responsibility for a choice my father had made to believe in me and the faith that my children had in me to provide for their stability. The tears and sobs came to the point I ran out of the house and through the gate into the pasture. At the time the only animals I had left were two goats and a retired race horse. One of the goats I had inherited when I bought the property, and the other, was a stray that showed up outside my pasture gate one morning so I simply just let her in. She remained with us until the end. Maggie, a former race horse, was a rescue of sorts that could be stand-offish, spooky and was usually difficult to manage.

I ran out of the house sobbing and fell against the safety of a grove of grandmother evergreens, as if they could absorb and support the weight of my failure and devastation. When I looked up through my grief and tears I was surrounded by these three four legged soul friends and found myself sitting under the shelter of the welcoming roots of support and guidance from the grandmothers evergreens I had been working so hard to ignore all along. Their patience whispered to me the longevity of the Universe and the truth of time and space. The goats had surrounded me on either side, laying their warm furry bodies around me and Maggie, the race horse, stood sentinel inches from my body, with her head tucked low down to the ground next to me. My animals carried a profoundly peaceful and compassionate space for me to unlock the river of unexpressed emotion I had buried so deeply inside me. Their eyes held wisdom and knowing, their fur held warmth and safety. With these soul friends I could finally let go and be swept away in the current of emotion. I cried tears of loss, tears of grief and tears of fear. I cried tears for all the years I hadn't cried at all. I cried for who I had become. I honestly can't say how long I stayed in the sacred space surrounded by the loving grace of the trees and my animals, but they simply just stayed with me and protected me for as long as it lasted. I felt grounded and loved. The moment the emotion stopped, and I made effort to control the genuine expression of what I was feeling, Maggie the horse looked me dead in the eye and bolted away. One by one, as if disgusted that the safe and beautiful space had ended, the goats ambled off after her and I was left alone again in my grief.

Days stretched into months and potential buyers came and went. At one point a family showed up that was "always going to write an offer," but delay after delay, never did. In truth, I didn't like them. They didn't feel right to me. I didn't want them to have my home. Perhaps it was me that ended that possibility agreement, one that could have ended the endless waiting. Maybe I just wasn't ready to let go. I was only moments away from the auction block of foreclosure when a family answered a sales post I had out in the internet world. It was a sunny day and for some reason, I felt very centered and peaceful. I got out to the property early and really stopped to take the time to feel, listen and communicate with this beautiful sacred land. For the first time in my life I could hear the wind on the wing of hummingbirds, I could see the mesmerizing sway of the blades of grass in the newly cut lawn. I said thank you to the Diva of the land for all that the experience of living there had brought me. I was ready to let go.

And the family showed up. They wrote an offer that was accepted by the bank in short sale, and the second mortgage promissory note binding my father was released. It was over. The family that showed up was a young family. One of their children was a foster child they were in the process of adopting. Possibility agreements turned into a promise and the choice of free will.

The Warrior and his Heartsong Bride...

I let the memories and the life lessons I learned with my Ranch wash over me as I gazed at Anamchara sleeping peacefully on his porch. As I took my first step towards him, he woke with a start as a huge sleepy grin spread across his face. He reached up and pulled me onto his lap.

Our first moment together again started in the same instantaneous second of awkwardness and immediate ease as the two other times I'd been with him before. The level of comfort, contentment and true spontaneous joy happened in an instant. We snuggled together under the warmth of the alpaca rug as the chilly breeze of winter licked across our faces. In the next moment I was lost again in his kiss. Our kisses hinted at a deeper knowing of each other, as did our eyes when they were locked together. Everything around me would disappear as the only thing in my consciousness was him. I still wasn't comfortable in those moments, and as much as I tried to look away could never quite break the gaze that held such promise and knowing in its power.

He invited me inside the ramshackle dwelling and what was lacking on the outside was forgotten instantly. In the center of the shack, carved out of the ceiling was a perfect circular dome sky-light. Old wood beams stretched from each of the walls connecting in perfect unison to the dome. Standing directly below this circle I was struck by a sense of the circular nature of all things and there in that moment, decided that it was the eye of

God. Warm, earthy wooden furniture and the deep rich aroma of sage and sweet grass lingered in the air creating an invitation to settle in and get comfortable. A beautiful wood stove filled his home with warmth and love. The entire space was one room and filled with totums and special momentos from floor to ceiling. Every direction my eye could focus was filled with things I wanted to touch, to smell – to understand. Most of the collection was Native American in origin, medicine bags, large stones and treasures from nature that felt alive and breathing in his space. The fireplace crackled quietly as we decided to leave for dinner.

As always, we found another amazing place to eat and it happened again, the stream of consciousness and connection between us like a river of exclusivity. So enraptured with each other, it was hard to see where one of us started and the other one ended. Laughter and joy came with conversation, one topic gliding effortlessly into another. The effortless stream between us was something I'd never experienced before. With Anamchara I felt completely acknowledged, seen and heard for exactly who and what I am. I felt beautiful beyond comparison and intelligent beyond measure. It was interesting to see people watching us in the rare moment that I was present enough to notice anyone besides him. Their looks were always wondering, about the intense man and his companion. I wonder if they saw what I felt, that Anamchara and I belonged together.

After conversation and connection so robust for our minds and spirits, it only took seconds outside the restaurant door for our bodies to act on the intensity and intimacy that we shared. We didn't even get the car doors closed completely before it was absolute desire, complete consumption and need, nothing mattered in that moment in time but coming together in the one song that never needs any words. Returning to his property we quickly found ourselves in front of the fireplace intertwined on the alpaca rug lain out to welcome us. We began our musical journey of the exquisite rapture of two people just hearing the melody with each other for the very first time. Moments of pure physical pleasure followed moments of intense pain. We shared a physical need for each other that often got rough and blistering. As the music poured out through the playlist, our passion changed and morphed to follow the flow.

    Clinging to him I got lost in a moment. Staring up through the eye of God, I saw clearly --two Indian lovers, together wrapped in pure bliss of their absolute knowing of each other. I saw their faces, I saw their truth, I saw their love. I was there with the lovers for one flicker of time and space. It was an odd knowing, but one I dismissed immediately. I shook off the sight and returned to the present moment, thoughts of the Indian lovers not returning again.

    We stayed up most of the night wrapped in each other's embrace talking about our life passions, hopes and dreams. Snuggled next to him, skin on skin I felt at home. When dawn finally rose we drifted off to sleep. Our partnership of sleep was a perfect fit, our bodies melted together as if they were two halves of the same whole. We had no blanket wars, and he didn't snore or thrash. There were no early morning interruptions from children wanting breakfast. For the first time, in a very long time I was a woman. I was simply me held in the arms of potential and promise. Brief flickers of what was possible burned brightly in my imagination. I loved the feel of his skin next to mine and his soft breath in my ear it whispered safety and the warmth of coming home.

    We spent the rest of the day laughing easily, sharing chocolate and beginning the dance of relationship. It was easy, it was natural and I felt the chains that had grown so hard and restrictive around my heart begin to loosen. He took me on a long and winding tour of his property and out to the corrals to meet his equine partners. He began sharing with me some of his values and goals for the spiritual program he was building. When we rounded the dirt road closest to the barn the herd of horses came galloping down the hillside to greet us. For me there is nothing like the majesty of watching horses gallop and play with manes flying and tails held high with power and conviction of the sheer pleasure in simply being alive. I finally noticed the beautiful black mare who had greeted me the day before. She stood off in the distance, away from the rest of the herd, her eyes still dancing wildly. "What is that mare's story?" I asked, feeling the residual effects of her greeting when I had arrived. "That's Satori. She's the lead mare around here. I call her my Dark Horse of mystery. Usually she stands separate from the herd, keeping watch. She's generally aloof and weary of strangers. That's part of her work here with the people who come. I've been doing a lot of work with her to become more socialized. She's the best horse I have when I work with people who are having trouble confronting their own fears." I certainly knew something about fear. What would the Dark Horse have to teach me I wondered silently, as we made our way back up toward his home.

With Anamchara I became viscerally aware of what it means to be fully present. When I was with him, I was fully absorbed in every single moment, every single conversation and every single touch. I began to see the shimmer of energy in the trees that surrounded us, food became alive and nourishing. I know this is the effect of the chemistry in "new love." It was the surreal feeling of everything becoming more alive and beautiful. I had lived in monochromatic simplicity for so long that the colors in spectrum became blinding in its comparison. That's the point. I have come to believe that the experience of "falling in love" and the presence and promise that is contained in those emotions and rapture is available to each of us, every single moment of every single day. In the beginning, I believed the world was simply a brighter place because I was sharing it with him. I didn't stop to think about this simple shift of me owning the presence, to only feeling it with another, was giving away my power. Giving away my Divine Truth that in this time and place, this human experience, I have the ability and the power to own that level of connection with every single living being around me. No, in the beginning it was all about him, all about the power and chemistry we brought to the table together. I had never tasted food so divine. I had never experienced chocolate for every single nuance of flavor that it boasted. I'd never laughed so heartily that every cell in my body felt the joy and release of pure happiness. Before him, I was walking dead in a sea of grey monotony.

The day faded into evening and we finally ventured out to a hot springs. We were mellow and reserved and enjoyed the respite of the water flowing around our battered hearts and souls. The weekend for me thus far had been a fairy tale. Idyllic, romantic and every single nuance of every hope and dream I had ever had for what I wanted in a relationship. Falling in love? I was falling, free falling. It had been so long, and my heart had been so numb for so long I felt like I had climbed out of the longest hibernation. I was hungry for connection and touch. I was starved for passion and right before my eyes Anamchara offered the possibility of having it all.

After dinner we began to drive. I noticed he was a little bit reserved and chalked it up to a long couple of days and an even longer night without much sleep. We started another one of our profound spiritual discussions that circled around "the sight." It is interesting to have a conversation with another human being that is so open to alternative realities. There are seers all around us. We are all seers. We all have the ability to tap into intuition, truth and realities that can't be explained by our traditional viewpoints of what it means to be human. I believe that part of what is happening on our planet today is that we as a species are starting to awaken to what we've always had the ability to do - to see. To see energy and to see the truth of the life-force that pulses through every living thing. It takes a courageous spirit to begin to walk down the road to open up to what's already there but can't be explained. I'd had some help. The Seer I had been working with for the last several months had begun to share with me some of my Divine Truth – through her third eye – the eye that we all have. In my awakening to my own Truth, I began to be aware, although still largely unconscious in my own ability to see for myself.

As we continued the conversation, we turned to the other side of being able to see – the dark side. Of course it exists. Where there is light, there is always dark. It's the yin and yang of the way our Universe works. I am a seeker of the light, there is no question. He talked about being in a few situations where the dark was called by people around him, times when he'd been exposed to dark elements and evil energy. It's easy to do and some more esoteric practices have ceremonies that can evoke the darkness that does exist around us. Because of these negative experiences he chose to close down his own ability to see. The conversation became more and more intense and he decided to pull the car over choosing to park under a beautiful grove of grandmother trees.

Then the conversation changed. It was as if the darkness we had been talking about in theory wrapped itself around us in the car. Anamchara's normally bright and energetic eyes became shrouded in clouds of confusion. His body closed down, his shoulders sagged and in a cold chill of foreboding I could feel the weight of something I couldn't explain. He said, "I have no idea where this is going between us. I always know when I start something with another person how long it's going to last. I always know if it'll be three weeks, three months or if it has the possibility of being something more. I have no idea where this is going with you. I can't see forever with you but I can't see period. I just can't see and I have no idea what that means. I don't know what you're meant to be to me."

Where in the hell did that come from? My river of emotion that had been held so tightly inside me threatened to spill over its banks. The Wicked Ego Witch started her dance of inadequacy and failure as the quiet tears of a lifetime of rejection began to flow. Nothing in the world had happened. In retrospect, it was a completely insane sentence, completely out of context. It was if he shifted and became someone or something different all together. I could feel the pull of his emotion and confusion. It was almost as if a lid of possibility and promise trying to close down – almost a warning sign, continue on if you dare.

I let the tears fall. Mostly because it had been so long since I had cried about anything that the release felt good. We talked about staying open to the journey and letting things just be what they were. Perhaps he could feel the energy and emotion that had gotten so intensely stirred up inside me. It wasn't like I had professed undying love or anything even remotely close. In the darkness, in my mind's eye I could see her again, the midnight mare Satori. Her eyes whipping wildly about as thunder and lightning crashed around her. The picture she showed me through my mind's eye was the Anamchara and his fear.

My Wicked Ego Witch rallied her battle cry and I was powerless to stop her. We had been here before and the writing was on the proverbial wall. She was bound and determined with her mental cruelty, powers and potions to do damage control. She raised her leather wrapped slender arm and with a crook of her red painted fingernails said, "That's it, we're finished here." All I could think about the rest of the ride home was that I was gone. I was not going to walk head-first into a broken heart with someone telling me upfront and honestly it was a real possibility. I was getting all my stuff and getting the hell away from him, and fast. When we pulled into his drive I was worked up to a fight or flight frenzy.

Then the shift happened again. We started talking. The energy around him changed and softened as if the clouds of his despair had been blown away. His shoulders raised and the sing song lilt of laughter returned to his voice. The kindness and compassion returned as if the veil of past had lifted and given way to the rainbow of the present. I wasn't so quick to follow but to engage my mind in a profound and powerful way is the surest path for me out of the darkness. We talked for hours and my anxiety level shrunk back to a place of comfort and ease. Anamchara started the music and asked if we could climb into bed. The passion flared again as we tumbled through another musical journey. He had put 'Last of the Mohicans' sound track on the stereo. The music is intensely raw and in some places down-right violent. As the music reached its crescendo, through a particularly intense musical set, the Indian lovers appeared to me again.

In a flash, I saw violence so swift and felt grief so overpowering that I winced viscerally with my entire body as if I could feel it myself, as if it was something I had experience before. Anamchara felt me shudder and asked what was wrong. The vision I had in my mind's eye was so powerful that I had no choice but to tell him. I saw war – a bloody battlefield, and a clash so violent that my whole body trembled in fear. The Warrior stood tortured and bloody, his body damaged and changed forever. And then I saw her, his Bride so grief stricken, and so emotionally shattered that she was broken in half. I saw the distance between them, as if they couldn't find their way back to each other. It was a flash. I saw it in my mind's eye but I felt the experience more than I saw, and then it was gone. The music streamed on and I begged Anamchara to turn it off. Something about the intensity of the soundtrack had awakened something deep inside me, as if it were a part of me somehow. It was something I couldn't ignore.

I slept fitfully and woke early the next morning.

While he slept, I walked outside to the safety and comfort of the trees and creek that surrounded us. In the distance I felt them, Radical Faith and Effortless Grace. The serenity and peaceful presence of their golden clothing felt like a cloak of protection surrounding me. I listened to the music of the creek rippling its babbling message of courage to stay open, stay present and stay connected to the journey. I was still shaken by what had happened the night before. Both in the completely out of context revelation that Anamchara didn't know what was happening for him between us, and then from the sight of the Indian lovers– whatever that was, whatever it meant. I had no clue. I doubted myself. Was it just a flight of fancy and an overactive imagination driven by music or maybe there was a scene like I'd seen in the movie and I just didn't remember it? There must be some rational explanation. Radical Faith stepped up beside me with her sword gleaming brightly against the morning sun and said loudly and clearly, "Trust what you know. Believe."

I was going to have to stay open, in a situation without the usual platitude of definition and see where the River decided to flow. Was the mother of all waterfalls straight ahead or the smooth waters of clear flow? Effortless Grace held up her jewel encrusted shield and asked me quietly to step back into my lifeboat.

Part of my difficulty with the morning was that my time with Anamchara was coming to an end. I couldn't really know if the end was just to the weekend or if our relationship was coming to an end permanently. All the fear I had felt prior to coming to him had completely disappeared and a new kind of fear had replaced it, the fear of loss and rejection. He had started to walk away the night before and something had happened that had changed the course. Partly it was a change in me. I had found a willingness to stay present and let things unfold. That was certainly a new place for me to find myself. I didn't leave when every part of me was screaming to do so. I stayed present and open and we came back together. But did we? It was almost as if something unseen and unknown was driving us both to stay open and continue rafting our lifeboats in the journey together.

My time was drawing swiftly to an end. I had to return home to my children. I have to say in full disclosure that I could have stayed there, in that place with him forever. I could have walked completely away from the life I had created – not walk away from my children, but gathered them up, and stayed with him forever. I had never been in a physical space that felt so full of love. I had never felt so seen and acknowledged. I felt emotionally supported in a way I had never had a man be willing to do before, even in the midst of his own fear and questioning. When he finally woke up, we began the dance of goodbye.

I was raised in the early 70's in the time of changing music. As I entered high school one band became the center of my universe. I was completely in love with Steve Perry of Journey. Thirty years later, I can still listen to every single song Journey ever produced and get lost in the music and often, I still do. Anamchara knows this about me and put Journey on the stereo as I began to gather my things to leave. The first song he played stopped me dead in my tracks. 'Send her My Love' off the Frontiers album. The words in the song are haunting, about a love journey that had come to an end. I asked him why he picked this particular song and he answered quietly, "It spoke to me." At that moment in time, I believed the dance we were doing was the dance of goodbye. The next song that came across was 'Faithfully.'

As the music played on the Indian lovers came to me again. I saw the Warrior—broken. His body had been horribly disfigured from the battle he had fought in. I saw the Bride, grief-stricken and alone, mourning his loss. I saw the miles of distance between them, as if the Warrior couldn't find peace with the fate that had befallen him.

And I saw his soul mate, his wife, all alone desperate in her waiting. Then it became so clear to me. They were real. I started calling them the Warrior and his Heart Song Bride. I pulled Anamchara close to me and began to tell the story of what I had seen. As I told the story, he began to cry. They were quiet tears of knowing. His energy was quiet and resigned as he listened to me describe all I had seen throughout our weekend together. I asked him if he could feel any resonance in the story I was telling him, did it feel real to him? He answered that he could feel something very real and very powerful but it didn't resonate inside his memory. I couldn't shake the feeling that there was something very powerful in this story. I had flashes that Anamchara and I were woven in this story somewhere but it didn't make any sense at the time. I'd never had any sight before – was this even real at all? I needed his confirmation. Surely he must feel something in the story if it was real. I could see glimmers of our truth, my Anamchara and I, contained in this story but it was so otherworldly I didn't have any perspective to put it in. The Wicked Ego Witch kept screaming about the little girl in me who just makes up too many stories. I didn't trust myself.

As I was getting ready to leave, Anamchara pulled me into a huge hug. I let myself melt into his embrace. As I closed my eyes I could see them again, the Warrior and his Heart Song bride. They were standing above us, together, smiling the most pure radiant smiles of beauty. I believed at the time we had released them, that somewhere, some karmic circle had been broken and that the lovers had reunited again. I could feel their peace. The truth of this was so profound I couldn't argue it. But why? Why had the lovers come to me? Who were they? What did it have to do with my relationship with Anamchara? Perhaps, I would never know.

As I was leaving, I left a note. On a small white piece of paper I wrote, "I will find you in the moonlight in another time and place." I kissed the paper leaving a lipstick print and placed it in a small box on a table that Anamchara used for his kitchen. It seemed obvious, the delicate box, which was filled with a stack of money. I put the note on top of the money, closed the lid and assumed that shortly after I left he would find it. And, after hugs and kisses, drove away and back into my life.

For me, there was something very disturbing about being jolted from one experience to another. When I got home I was thrust back into the reality of my life with my kids. Who was I going to be now? I knew that I was forever changed as a result after the weekend, I knew that for me things could never be the same. I'd felt too much, opened myself to emotion, to beauty and to pain. I had moved through my own fears and sucked up enough courage to keep moving forward when every ounce of me was screaming to turn back. The walls around my heart that had grown so thick and unyielding had started to collapse. I felt raw and vulnerable, exposed and quivering. I had to suck it up and return to the land of the life, I had created before the Anamchara.

When I finally walked in my front door, my life as single mother and sole provider hit me like a tidal wave. The overwhelming sameness of everything in my life, returned with a fury. How was I going to balance falling in love with the responsibilities I had to my children and my life? I hadn't slept much at all, for the entire weekend. I was still swirling in the altered reality of the pure bliss I had experienced much of the weekend. I had faced my own terror and fear and went in the first place. I had allowed myself to be completely present in each and every moment that presented itself. I had gone from the top of the world, to the valley and back up again. On the journey I had found the Warrior and his Bride. On the journey I had found the center of myself. Who was I going to be back in my own reality?

I just wanted to be alone. I wanted to stay lost in that

world with my Anamchara. I wanted to sleep. I wanted my kids and my responsibilities to just go away – at least long enough so that I could put everything I'd just experienced into some sort of manageable box. It was the rudest transition. I needed time to think and to process and what I got was sleep deprivation and demands.

The phone rang fairly early the night I returned home, at least in Anamchara's timing of things and I got lost again in his voice. He said he was still surrounded by my energy and that he was languishing in the afterglow of our weekend together – like I'd never left. It seemed like a weird thing to say after his non-committal distance in the end, but I was hungry for the connection so I accepted his glow and basked in it awhile longer.

One of the interesting transitions to waking up in my own life was that I started to realize how many things I had stopped doing. I have always loved to write. Writing for me is the catharsis of my soul. Trapped in a whirlwind of crazy emotions I picked up pen in hand and started to write again in a journal that I had left covered with the dust of neglect. I needed to organize my thoughts about what had just happened. I am not one to wax poetic, but on this first night back into my real life I tried to stretch myself a little bit as I wrote about the weekend Anamchara and I had shared.

It was every sunrise I have ever seen in hopeful possibility.
It was every sunset I've ever watched in sorrowful passing of the brilliant colors of light and dark that it shares with those patient enough to watch from beginning to end.
It was every ray of sunshine that warmed my soul.
It was every piece of chocolate that is savored and shared.
It was every drop of rain that washes away - the rain of the soul, the tears of the heart -- for past, for present and for possibilities of the future.
It was every laugh that had every cell in my body open and ready for more.

It was every kiss I have ever experienced.
It was every part of my body -- alive and on fire -- literally and metaphorically.
It was every horse ride I've wanted to experience wild and free -- fully in the moment, fully trusting in complete and total partnership - becoming one flying through the night.
It was every fear, every scary dream and every realization that the fears were unfounded and that indeed the dream was just imagination.
It was every primal desire of the full moon - full of mysticism and magic, fairy tale and ceremony.
It was the circle of life in a moment in time shared by a man and a woman full of passion and desire.
It was beautiful
It was profound
It was healing
It was calling to a higher place and to a destiny yet unclear
It was fully connected and shared completely
It will never be forgotten or diminished in its power
It just was.

That was the truth of the entire experience. It was every nuance on the continuum, with every ray of hope and possibility attached to it. What I didn't know was whether I'd ever see him, or experience anything with him again. I felt both emptiness and fullness all at the same time. I ached for the thought of not having him in my life, but I felt a rich expansiveness I'd never experienced before. I just had to stay open and let things be what they were which was a very difficult task for a woman who had always based her life on schedules, control and outcomes. A new stretch in the River had opened up, it was up to me to say yes and follow its flow.

The days rolled on and while Anamchara didn't call, other things that hinted at a new way of living for me began to happen. I started to play the piano again. I started looking at my children and really seeing them – who they are – the spirits that are uniquely theirs. I laughed more and felt myself start to open and move closer to the Truth that has always been who I am – the part of me that had gotten lost long ago.

The weekend had been utterly profound. It felt as though a window to me, that had been closed for so long, finally opened to expose the radiant sunshine of life. I needed to talk to my Seer again. I had been thrown off guard by the connection that I felt Anamchara and I shared, and then again with my visions of the Warrior and his Bride. I felt a little crazy actually, like perhaps my imagination was working overtime. I needed to understand the Truth from the perspective that only she could give me.

1/24/2009 The phone call with the Seer opened as always, with a prayer for the highest and greatest good of understanding to occur. We immediately moved into the space of knowing and we started with the question that I always ask first.

What do you see in my space, what is it my soul wants me to see about this time?" She answered, "A butterfly emerging from a growth period of tremendous energy. There has significant clearing of chaos. You have ended some agreements and set intentions. You are holding the space for yourself of spiritual awareness. What you no longer need is falling away. It's taken the whirlwind of chaos to clear it off. You allowed yourself to trust the process, to stay with it. You've gotten a taste of the power that you are as a spiritual being. This is a shore of a new land and you are standing on a gorgeous beach. How do I do this, is your question. The body personality doesn't know – but the spirit does. Trust spirit. Be powerful and focus on your intention. You feel vulnerable and exposed. There are no filters between yourself and the world. You have an incredible skills set to get you through the process. Use the tools you have – it becomes lighter and quicker. Clarify what space is yours to occupy, have compassion – don't take on what isn't yours. Look at where your energy is with others."

I asked her about the weekend that I'd just experienced and this is what she said. *"You are two souls who have been on the planet before. Your original home world is in another dimension. You have the same energy signature. There is a HUGE hello from your souls' very essences. The experience was amazing, real it was. You both had a reaction to the connection – glimpses into other spaces. How big and powerful it was. You are blowing up old mind pictures and beginning to release paradigms that are limiting. You are learning to trust more and more. You are both having experiences of living and healing and releasing thought processes that have kept you encased. Your ability to see is expanding. You are both followed by a collection of souls, overseers or guides that are holding space. They are choosing to come through at this particular time. Your challenge is to support each other in who you are. This could show up very differently than you expect. Explore different ways of being.*

I asked her to enter the Anamchara's space and tell me what she saw there. I feel compelled to mention that I had his permission to do this. It would be unthinkable to me to enter another person's fifth dimensional space without their permission to do so. And I honestly believe that if a person were resistant to the sight of another, he could close down the window to the view.

Her view of Anamchara was unrestricted and her response was immediate. *"There is a huge hello from him. The experience was amazing for him as well. He feels a lightness of being and a new space being opened up. He is blessed and thankful for the soul agreement it feels very rich to him."*

I asked her what I needed to see and she responded, *"In spirit, we are ultimately one. The energy of the relationship is about opening heart space. It's so beautiful, it's almost painful. To resist the fullness would equal pain. We are beings of pure love." She also said which I found out of context at the moment, "You are bigger than your story – don't minimize, don't qualify. Be clear with your intentions."*

Anamchara finally called about a week later and apologized profusely for the delay in communication. He'd had some crisis happen in his business life that took up most of his time. We'd sent a few emails back and forth so I knew he was still engaged in moving forward but hearing his voice is what I desperately needed. I was feeling very insecure based on our last night together and because the Wicked Ego Witch had started working overtime to keep me bound in feelings of inadequacy and loss, I was struggling to stay grounded and centered in allowing the relationship to progress on its own terms.

A day or so after I left the first weekend, I sat down and wrote a letter, perhaps the better explanation is that the letter with the story, told itself. It was written for Anamchara from the perspective I'd come to believe at the time, about the Warrior and his Bride. What is interesting to me is that without knowledge of what the definition of the word Anamchara meant at the time, I chose to start calling him by this name.

The Warrior and his Heart Song Bride:

Anamchara,

As usual, my gift and curse of vision and clarity has caused many moments of confusion and questioning about the meaning of our union. Was there supposed to be any meaning at all? I know there was, there is and will continue to be. We began a journey of the soul together, to co-create as we go along in the sacred space of possibility, unattached to outcome, a place of brightly colored hues and deep reserves of grey.

I say today apologetically that I was lost in my own sea, my own sea of emotion, of time and space, of connec-

tion and presence, a place I had never been before. I was so lost in my sea of selfishness that I was too overwhelmed to see the other side of the story, your side.

It's been a long and winding process of memories, feelings and reflection to be able to say your story and process were not lost in my self-absorption.

I didn't stop to reflect, only felt in wild abandon. I missed the subtle shadows behind your eyes, the hesitation in your completion of our union and the slight crackle in your voice as we shared intimate conversation about your past, a past that is vivid in its implication to your life.

You spoke of being closed to the sight, of not finding clarity on your vision, and how you fear the dance of the seven days with the dark feminine.

In your eyes, through your tears, you showed the clarity behind the story I was told by the broken warrior and his heart song bride. It wasn't my story. Although I felt her terror and the pain she carried to the end of her days of longing and grief for her warrior. I felt her healing as she completed her karma by knowing her lover really never left her side. He was only too trapped by his brokenness and his loss of faith in his love for her to find her again in that lifetime. It was your story. The story your soul spoke to me in those moments, the ones of gentle love, the ones of raw power and the ones of loss. It's in those moments that the circle of their lifetime connected. It is a start for you, in knowing their story. It holds the opportunity for you to end the cycle of trying to heal your own brokenness by giving your heart only to those that are broken. It was a start for me to hold the sacred space of possibility for you.

You must find your sight again. You must trust that the road you have chosen and the souls that you chose to create with were the right choice at the right time. You must let go of the trauma that has confined you, both by choice and by destiny. You must dance with the dark feminine and allow her to speak to you, for in doing so you will find your heart song again. You must have radical faith.

You came to me, you chose me. Your soul knew that the next step on the journey was to connect with another powerful spirit who could help you see what you choose not to. It was my choice to meet the destiny head on and ride the ebb and flow of the co-creation.

I hold safe space and good healing energy for you. I hold the pain and fear in sacred honor so that you might have the courage to move through it on your own. I hold the brokenness in pure radiant light so that it may be completed. I return the gift you gave so beautifully to me. Dance with the dark feminine when the time comes. She waits.

Several months before I met him, I had come across a Celtic phrase that I thought was beautiful called Anam Chara. Anam Chara in its literal Celtic definition means 'soul friend.' When I found the word, something moved deep and powerfully within me. I started using the word often when I wrote to him. I hadn't done any further research to figure out what Anam Chara really meant but from near the very beginning of my time with this magical man, would often call him my Anamchara.

John O'Donohue in his gorgeously rich, deeply spiritual book, "Anam Cara: A Book of Celtic Wisdom" describes an Anam Chara relationship powerfully. When I came upon his book, and began to read its pages, I came to believe that this was the type of experience I was having in my relationship. Everything about what we shared was moving me to an inner depth inside me and because of the spiritual connection we shared with each other I found a place of Truth I knew could never be destroyed. There is no guarantee in this tradition about the length of time an Anam Chara relationship will last. Only that its origin and depth is at the level of the soul.

The Anam Chara relationship as I've come to understand it, and as I tried to experience it, isn't easy. It's raw, powerful and vulnerable. For me it was a truly scary thing to be that intimately open with another, particularly in learning to navigate a love relationship. So much of what the Anamchara and I shared had started to become this very circular thing. The depth of connection was addictive, and through it, layers of my Self were being revealed. But interestingly enough, there was a protective safety about its quality. It was as if we shared a magical space, where time stood still and we could be exactly who we were in all our facets.

Very often when I write I simply fall unconscious. My mind goes quiet and my fingers just move with the spirit that flows from within me. The words just come out and I've learned to honor their flow. When I wrote the story of the Warrior and the Bride for Anamchara I had no idea of its significance. Writing for me is almost channeling, my spirit takes over. It would happen over and over again in emails that I would write to him. Something would just come into my consciousness and I'd send another email. He would come to tell me that my emails would speak to him profoundly of things he was going through at the time that he read them. When I wrote the story of the Warrior what I didn't realize at the time was how the story would unfold its truth and significance as my relationship with Anamchara would follow its flow.

I was starting to learn the dance of timing, of balance and of the give and take that happens when two souls agree to take a journey together. I had started learning this dance several months before with an entirely different kind of soul and what she had to teach me would serve me well in what was to come with Anamchara in my journey to heart space.

Soul Sisters...

Just the word horse can take me from the depth of human despair and self-imposed misery to the height of passion in a syllable. It is every single nuance of these magical creatures that has held me captive since early childhood. Their movement inspires music in my heart in those sacred spaces where pure peace and true harmony reside. The musk of the barn, mud on my boots and the sweet smell of freshly bailed hay is pure salvation in those moments when my life had become a precarious balance of pure hilarity or insanity, often one in spite of the other. In the barn it is neither laugh nor cry but often times both and occasionally, at the same time. In me, horses evoke every single human emotion, some more often and intense than others – like fear for example, and through fear I would find pure joy and the path to oneness that can be found in true partnership with another soul. This soul sister on my journey showed up in a four legged body of chestnut, which, with just the right amount of sun light, radiates gold.

I had one thing of "value" left from my days at the Ranch. For some reason, perhaps as a token of all the miles I had meditated behind the wheel, I had kept my virtually new riding lawnmower. One day I got this little intuition that maybe I could trade my riding mower for another horse. It was time. I needed something that was just mine. The Universe will always answer when you set out a clear intention, always. Just as I made my intentions clear, my Dixie showed up, and she showed up in an internet ad saying "Looking to trade quarter horse mare for a riding lawnmower." Oddly enough, she turned out to be located just a short walk through a Christmas tree farm from where I had decided I wanted to board my horse.

When I first met Dixie, it was a comedy of errors. The young couple that had her for sale were literally on the last day of tenancy in their property and that evening Dixie was scheduled to be moved to their new property a long distance away. Earlier in that day I had taken the drive out to the barn that I was hoping would be a good match for me, hoping the couple would call me so I could see the horse I was interested in from the ad. I didn't receive the phone call until I was long back home. On a whim I decided to turn around and go back. When I first saw my horse she was galloping frantically around a smaller pasture area. She was hard to catch and not cooperative. When the husband saddled her up and climbed on, she crow hopped down the driveway.

That should have been enough. I do not like difficult horses. Standing in my own truth I must admit I am probably afraid of horses. I am afraid of being out of control and being thrown. I would never knowingly climb on a horse that I knew for a fact had a history of crow hopping with its owner. I saw this happen with my own eyes. Why I said, "Ok, I'll take her," is to this day a complete mystery. She scared me to death.

We traded straight across, my lawnmower for Dixie and the deal was done. Now it was time for me to figure out what I was going to do with her. For some reason, I started slow. I took a lot of time just hanging out with her, nothing to do, nowhere to go. In honest reflection it's likely that I was simply stuck in fear. We spent the first several days together with me just trying to catch her in the enormous pasture where she lived. I would get frustrated and angry, chase her around, run her off and then just stop and walk away. I could almost hear her faint giggles as I stomped out of the pasture vowing to sell her the next day.

Bursting at the seams with frustration and self-doubt I would stand at the gate just watching her. Even for her aloofness, she would stand close enough, almost within reach of my arm with just her hind towards me. Then she would amble off, stopping to pull at a random clump of grass scattered haphazardly around the pasture. Swinging her whole body to face me, she would stare at me with deep soulful eyes that seemed to whisper, "That which is important enough, takes whatever time it takes. Slow down." And she would quietly disappear into the herd of pasture mates that stood waiting for her off in the distance.

I hated being in the beginner's mind. That place of

utter confounding confusion. As an adult and I guess at the time as a "human" vs. "beast of burden" I thought I was just supposed to know what to do with her. I'd had horses at my Ranch, all of whom depended on me and seemed to love me in their own ways. I didn't have to take care of Dixie, at least not in the everyday way I had to do at the Ranch. It was up to me to suck it up and figure it out walking through the fires of fear every step of the way.

Dixie is an old soul. You can see the depths of eternity in her huge brown eyes. If you listen close enough, she has a story to tell – about humanity, about relationships—about family. She speaks of learning to trust, of taking time and of being truly present and committed to the process, not the outcome.

We finally crossed the threshold of my own fear as I grabbed slivers of courage enough to climb on her back. She didn't make it easy on me either. She demanded my focus and concentration. She demanded respect and her own dignity. She drew her boundaries and challenged me to draw mine. It took enormous commitment from me to keep fighting through my own fears: the fears of failure, inadequacy, of being in the beginner's mind and trying to pretend as an adult that I knew so much more than I did. I've always been able to fake my way through anything, but I could not fake my relationship with Dixie. She would not allow it. It was as if she beckoned to my soul to dig in, dig deep and face myself. This was and continues to be huge challenge for me. There were days when I just had enough and thought I'd made the wrong choice in trading for her but the voice of Radical Faith inside me said, "Stay true. Commit."

Dixie has never so much as offered to do anything, in any way that would ever hurt me. She has never even thought about crow hopping, or biting or kicking me. Little by little, we both faced our own wariness of the other. I have no idea of Dixie's past. I know she has trust issues, just like I do. I know that it took a lot of time, and a lot of consistency (in addition to a whole lot of mistakes) to gain her trust. I know to the depths of my soul she would never, ever hurt me in any way, something I had never known with any other being in my entire life. It was the start of trust, the start of trusting myself to do the right things, be present and be honest and be good enough – just exactly as I am.

Little by little we built a relationship. I had to give, she had to give. I'd draw a boundary and she'd step a little closer. She'd draw a boundary and I'd back a little bit away. I had no idea Dixie was teaching me the dance of intimacy, the dance of relationship. My relationship with Dixie is honestly the first relationship I've ever had where I've been asked to be completely who and what I am. I could bring no false pretenses, bring no lies. I could only bring myself. With Dixie, the Wicked Ego Witch was quiet. Perhaps she's just as fascinated with this incredible creature as I am.

Dixie opened the door to what is possible in Heart Space. I was ready again. I stated my intention loudly and clearly to the Universe. I was ready for "My One." And the Universe answered. It always does.

The King of Broken Hearts....

Anamchara and I continued conversations by phone and they remained connected, passionate and full of hope and promise. We started delicately navigating our way through our relationship stories of the past. He would talk in a voice so deep and so full of regret for the women who had come before me. He talked about failed promises, of poor relationship choices and of the relationship that was supposed to have lasted forever. When the Anamchara loves he would tell me, he loves forever. It might be a long, hard road to get there, but once he did, the mark on his soul would remain forever. That was pretty heady stuff for a girl desperately seeking the one man who would love her no matter what she'd done or for what she feared she might do again. I knew myself too well. I was always eager to jump off the cliff of love anxious and ready to pull the parachute that would end the possibility long before the thrill of accomplishment could actually become reality.

One evening, we started talking about our agreement to stay open to the possibilities and in the same conversation he started talking about breaking my heart. "I just don't want to break your heart," he would say. "I honestly don't have any sense of where this is going between us. You've known all along I am looking for my life-partner so until I know something more, I am going to stay open to whatever comes along." Perhaps I should have been paying more attention to the carefully chosen words he used to tell me what I refused to hear verbatim. I would quietly reassure him that I felt comfortable seeing to my own heart, and would say repeatedly to him over the course of time to come, "Trust me to know my own heart, no matter what happens." The only boundary I spoke out loud was that if he decided to start seeing someone else, I wanted to have the courtesy of knowing immediately. Trust me to know my own heart? I was still having trouble registering heartbeats at all. It was kind of like suggesting that I could be trusted to run the Boston Marathon without knowing at all how to walk. But somewhere in the quiet recesses of my very essence I could hear Radical Faith whispering, "Hang on. Stay in the River. It will be worth it."

Some might say this is a man's cleaver attempt to have kept his woman quietly at bay. Generally speaking, and with any other man, in any other circumstance I would agree completely. But our relationship kept moving forward with such a level of integrity, emotional honesty and open communication that I trusted the Anamchara at his word. That's not to say my little green monster didn't rear her head from time to time, nor does it mean I walked blindly without paying attention to the sign posts along the way. I wonder how often we ignore those very sign posts as we make our way through the rapids in the journey of relationship.

We made plans to spend another night together only a couple weeks after the first. I couldn't wait to be in his space again. I had grown to love his ramshackle cottage in the desert. It felt like my own private oasis from the world and I hungered to be there, to stay there with him, forever.

It would catch me off guard, in the first moments we came together, the flash of fear that would always find me. Then in the moment that followed I'd find the simple knowing of pure peace and connection that we would find with each other. We went out for another spectacular dinner, where kismet led the way. We left his house with our destination unknown right up until the point I said, "Here, pull over here…" We ended up at a Japanese steakhouse, the kind where they cook the meal right at your table. What strikes me most about this dinner was the fact that we were completely surrounded by people at our table, and again, the world shifted to the microcosm of just being the two of us. We had our legs wrapped around each other, telling stories, my glass of wine flowing freely – well, until he decided to order quail eggs. To this day I still gag at the thought. Disgust turned into hysterical laugher as we continued to alienate the world around us.

Dinner gave way to passion as we left the restaurant and made our way through the high desert roads back to his home. As we pulled into the drive, his herd of horses grazed quietly in the light of the full moon. A feeling of profound peace radiated from their very beings. The black horse Satori grazed quietly next to a late fall foal, her body angled in a protective stance to guard the little one against the unknown. In her relaxation, I too could take a deep breath and let the rest of our night unfold before me. We found ourselves in the warmth and glow of his fireplace and snuggled in next to each other. For some reason as we lay snuggled up together he was much more open about his thoughts for me. He would mutter under his breath that I had it all, everything he was looking for, that maybe he could see a future for us together. I never commented on his mutterings, I don't think he knew he actually spoke them out loud. We traveled through another musical journey together, wrapped tightly in body, mind and spirit on the alpaca rug. Just as we drifted off to sleep, a doorway to another time and place opened just briefly, for Anamchara. He had a vision, of us together – somewhere surrounded by a high wall, my long hair blowing in the wind. It was just as he was drifting off to sleep, but he was awake enough, with me snuggled deep into his chest to speak the vision, quietly and beautifully into my ear. He had opened to the sight, even if for only one small moment in time.

I am an early riser, while Anamchara, usually up all night and can easily sleep late into the day. By then I'd come to appreciate the simple solace in the mornings while he lay sleeping. I powered up his computer and got ready to check my email. He frequently leaves about a million screens open on his computer and that is no exaggeration. I started minimizing screens and one simple sentence in an email left open on his screen scorched into my consciousness.

Several months before me, Anamchara had been involved in a serious relationship. He had told me about her and the relationship they shared and I guess in full disclosure he had mentioned that she sent still sent him emails from time to time. Perhaps it was the casual way he mentioned her that made it comfortable for me to dismiss the significance of any remaining emotions they might have shared. The sentence in her latest email had me reeling and doubting anything and everything that had ever been spoken to me by this man.

In a rare burst of supreme composure I turned on

the coffee pot to make his first cup, which considering that I don't drink coffee is pretty magnanimous. I walked around in circles as the pot percolated and dripped second by second, trying to decide if I was going to grab my things and just go. It was a 90/10 debate – 90% just leave. I tapped into what I call the "freeze zone" where emotion doesn't reside, and when the last drop of the fresh brew slowly found its way into the carafe, I poured his cup, walked over to the bed and said, "You need to get up… now."

One eye at a time he flinched open. "Is something wrong?" I responded with an ice cold chill that left no room for imagination and replied, "I am going to give you the courtesy of your coffee and then we'll talk." He flew out of bed and I simply pointed him to the computer screen. "I wasn't snooping through your computer, I was trying to minimize screens so I could find the internet icon on your desktop and apparently you left this email open." As he read, I walked out his door leaving it to slam behind me.

I walked down to the creek. I got as quiet as I could so I could try to get a sense of what my truth really was. Honestly, I didn't know why I was still there at all. I did the best I could to breathe and get centered. The trees surrounded me in a protective space that begged me to remember longevity and wisdom of time. I offered prayers, mostly out of desperation, to give me the words to say when it was time to walk back inside. I felt the sword and shield of Faith and Grace quietly offer up their courage and blessing. In those quiet moments of desperation, I felt the urge to stay open and let things unfold. Given the circumstances and my past this seems miraculous in retrospect, and I have plenty of ex-relationships who would easily attest that scenes like this would have normally sent any smart man running for cover. I had handled myself with a grace and courage I didn't know I was capable of. When I walked back inside he said, "Sit down, read this, please." I burst into tears and refused to read anything further telling him that it wasn't any of my business to intrude upon words that had been written to him by someone that he loved. His voice became so small and so sincere he almost sounded desperate, "Please, just read this."

Crying, I sat down and looked at the screen, as he walked out the front door. The day before my arrival his former lover had written him another email apologizing for the first email I had found by accident. In her email she talked about missing him but said that she was clear that he had told her he was trying to move on. Her words were so eloquent, so full of poise and emotion that I simply cried harder. They were words that I was sure I could have written. It broke my heart. I sat quietly at the computer screen lost in my own thoughts when Anamchara walked back into the house. Looking over at him I saw a man torn by emotion and afraid of losing someone that he cared about, I guess at the time what I thought I saw was his worry that he might lose me.

There are spontaneous moments you can go right instead of left or change your mind in the middle to follow the quiet intuition that says, do the impossible, it's worth it. This was one of those moments. I had a choice to make. Every bit of relationship history I had was screaming at me to leave, leave now and never look back. Did I trust him? In truth, no I did not, not in that moment in time. The only thing that saved our journey together was the odd coincidence that the woman had sent another email to him in apology and regret for the first email I had accidentally stumbled across.

I will always look back at that moment in time as Divine Grace. It was that crossroads where we could have ended, where my fears of loss, inadequacy and shame could have overwhelmed me to the point I would not have found the courage to move forward.

The Beating of my Heart...

I had been having chest pains on and off for the past couple of years. Twice these pains had landed me in the ER. Part of the beauty and curse of being reunited with my birth family is that I now understood my family medical history, a family history riddled with heart disease at a very young age. Being only 40, physicians took a light approach to my complaints but did all the basic and usual tests to rule out heart disease. Every test that was ordered came back negative. My cardiologist finally said to me, "Well, there's one way to know for sure. Do an angiogram." Having an invasive cardiac procedure where a catheter would be threaded up through my femoral artery into my heart was absolutely not on my must do list. The cardiologist in a moment of spoken brilliance said in passing that I could spend my life never knowing and running in and out of the hospital, or wouldn't it be easier to do the angiogram and just know? With that rationalization, the angiogram was scheduled for a week later.

I knew when I scheduled the angiogram that it fell on a day Anamchara would normally be off work. I knew beyond a shadow of a doubt that I needed him to be there with me. The bottom line was that I felt safe, and loved with him beside me. When we were together the combination of our energy and his spiritual practices created an environment of complete protection, peace and serenity for me. He has the most remarkable ability to hold emotional space in a way that made me feel genuinely supported. It is a true gift. I knew his levity would wash away my fears. I knew his ability to pray would be held throughout my entire procedure. And I was counting on his prayers to help me wake up from the procedure and return to my life.

After the drama of the morning and with our time together quickly coming to an end, I took a huge risk. Wrapped tightly in his embrace I whispered quietly in his ear, "I'm having a little bit of heart surgery on Thursday and I really wish you would be there with me." He jolted away from me, "Heart surgery? What are you talking about, what do you mean?" I explained what was happening and then asked him gently if he'd be willing to come up to be with me. I have a hard time asking for what I need. I am always afraid the answer will be no. He sighed softly and said yes.

The day before the procedure I fell into a place of complete fear. I was absolutely certain that I was going to die on the table during the angiogram. It is weird what happens when you believe you're going to die. I simply got very focused. I cleaned every nook and cranny of my entire house. I made lists of bank account numbers, telephone numbers and life insurance policies. I wrote notes to my children and tried to take stock of the life I had lived. Had it been worth it? I can't say I ever came to a clear answer. I knew I'd done the best I knew how to take care of my children. I'd been as generous as I knew how to be to those people around me but had I really ever loved? Had I ever opened my heart completely and said yes, come what may to all that life has to offer? No. No, I had not. I started bargaining with the Universe. I said out loud, "Please, if I can just live through this I promise I'll learn to love. I promise I'll open my heart and love my children more and do better with what I've been given. I just need another chance, a chance to open my heart." At the time I didn't see the connection between the prayers that I offered and the fact that I was getting ready to undergo a procedure to investigate the inner anatomy of my heart – was it blocked in a physical way? What was causing the chest pain?

Anamchara arrived at my house late the night before my procedure. As we climbed into my bed as he muttered again, that I was the entire package for him – body, mind, heart and soul – the four directions of balance in the sacred hoop of life. It's always funny to me when he mutters out loud and doesn't realize he's doing it. We spent the early morning hours in each other's passionate embrace, just as we'd both drifted off to sleep, the alarm rang. It was time. I took a deep breath of courage and kissed my children goodbye.

From the moment we walked into the hospital it was like he became my protector and muse. He had me laughing hysterically, teased into a sexual frenzy and kissed so soundly that every nurse on the cardiac cath lab floor probably is still talking about it. I will never quite look at a hospital gown the same again. We kissed for the hours leading up to pre-op. Every time a nurse walked in she would have to politely cough to interrupt us. I have to say, there was no fear. My fear was completely gone. When they came in to wheel me to the procedure I was absolutely emotionally fine. Anamchara stood right beside me, holding my heart space while I could not. He held me in sacred prayer, goodness and light. I could feel it radiating between us. I have never felt so completely at peace and confident of any outcome. Lots of drugs later I emerged from the procedure to see his face again and was given the news that I have a completely normal, functioning heart.

Part of the recovery process following an angiogram is that the patient has to lay completely still for three hours so the femoral artery has time to seal off after the invasion of the catheter tubing. As I was wheeled back into my recovery room I only had one demand. I wanted Anamchara to climb onto the gurney and sleep next to me. He hesitated only long enough for me to shoot him a look of absolute sincerity and he climbed in next to me. We both slept, side by side for the next three hours. I woke and left the hospital without so much as a tiny pinprick from where the procedure might have been.

What became most interesting to me is that from that moment on, I've hardly had even a slight tinge of chest pain. Is it simply an interesting coincidence that I began to remove the emotional restraints I had placed around my heart and began to feel the emotions I needed to feel that the chest pain ended? I wonder if my physical chest pain symptoms were the result of my body's insistent message to open up, pay attention and start living while I still have time.

Paying attention...

What is so extraordinary to me on this journey is what started happening to me. I began to really look at my behavior in context of a romantic relationship. I started looking at all the patterns that were so engrained in who I am in partnership. I have this tendency to "get lost." I begin to get very absorbed in my partner's life, his work, his interests. The only way I knew how to be engaged and remain interested was if I had something to do, or to be. I had never had the experience of having intense emotions for a man, and staying true to my own life and own responsibilities. The key distinction in that sentence is "intense" emotion. I had been in plenty of relationships where I was my own sovereign country. I did my thing, didn't get involved and frankly just didn't care what my partner was doing or where he was going. It was the result of the mountain of ice I'd built around my heart. I was afraid of my own patterns. I was afraid of getting so lost in another that I would lose my own way and in full disclosure, the end was always looming on my emotional horizon as just another gift from my Wicked Ego Witch. Every time I'd ever taken a romantic fall, the end was always devastating, and it was devastating because, I'd give myself so completely, change and morph so entirely, that I would lose my very essence inside the man I was with. When he left, and he always did, I'd send myself right along with him.

I began to be intellectually aware of this pattern as I was moving through the motions of building a relationship with Anamchara. I started noticing what was happening inside me. Emotions that I hadn't felt in decades started to come to the surface and demand their due. It's a slippery slope, at least for me, to start feeling. I finally realized one day that emotion to me was a verb. It was a thing of action. To feel something, I had to do something. More often than not, that action was destructive. I hadn't learned to sit quietly with emotions, nor had I learned that emotion is transient. The last relationship I had been in, where there was intense emotion I was completely out of control. I did horrendous, shameful things (according to the Ego Witch anyway) and I was mortally afraid to open the Pandora's box of intense negative emotion. I was afraid of what I might do, of who I might become. I had taught myself over the course of my life that I couldn't be trusted to feel.

As the emotional insights revealed themselves I could watch myself as an observer of "me." It would feel like I was watching myself, from a balcony or terrace as I'd say something or do something and fight to stay in control. I think I did a pretty decent job of keeping my emotional turmoil hidden, at least at face value from Anamchara. He is an extremely intuitive man, and very energetically connected to me. It would be a gross misrepresentation of him to assume that he couldn't feel what was going on, my guess is that if he was paying any attention, he could, but he never commented on it. I am a master at deflecting conversation away from myself and back onto my partner. Perhaps it's my social work background. As he would often say, "You have this habit of asking the most inane questions, but, I love your inane questions because they make me think." It was always my way of masterfully evading the possibility of revealing too much of myself. I was always terrified in relationships that my partner would see the real me, whomever that might have been and leave based on what they saw. The Wicked Ego Witch exercised ironclad control over this, and I was powerless to stop her, even if I tried. I was beginning to uncover and examine the emotional work I had to do to open my Heart Space and step more fully into the Divine Truth that I am. It's one thing to begin to see who and what you are. It's quite another to be living in the moment and make a choice to do something different. It's part of the journey.

As I started sorting through the newly uncovered wreckage yard of my emotions, I started taking a hard look at where I was in my life. I had lived without personal passion for so long I simply couldn't answer the question, "Who am I and what do I want to contribute in this lifetime?" My relationship with Anamchara started to challenge my core beliefs about everything I stood for. He is a very passionate, mission driven man. He has nurtured his vision to build stronger youth through spiritual practices for as long as he can remember. As he talked about his work partnering horses and people together I was captivated. I'd always believed in the power of horses, particularly after my experiences with my mare Dixie. She had taught me more than any human about boundaries, trust and respect. She taught me how to move through my fear and limitation pictures that were impacting my entire life. What I couldn't understand about the Anamchara was what was taking so long? He seemed stuck in making things happen. He was doing some small interactive groups with horses and at-risk youth but it seemed painfully slow to me who can be such a force in making things happen quickly. I was ridiculously attracted to this aspect of him because it posed such a different long view of the world and how our gifts and talents are supposed to manifest. I am a very specific, time bound visionary and if I can't make it happen, like right now or tomorrow, I am likely to move on to something else. Luckily I am a very powerful person and have this crazy ability to manifest the impossible. My problem has always been staying satisfied with what I manifested long enough to make it worth the effort. I had no concept of staying power. I had no concept of nurturing and loving attentiveness without attachment to a particular outcome. I was beginning to learn the lessons of nurturing, of slowing down, of taking the time to plan and of letting things take the time they needed to take.

Anamchara and I would bump right into the circular nature of manifestation many times in our relationship. We would learn how our very different natures would both challenge and enhance our partnership together. We fit together that way, like the yin and yang of things – where I am strong, he needs work and where he is strong, I could use a swift kick in the ass. He taught me many things about slowing down, being patient and trusting the Universe to guide the way.

Intention....

I had learned about the power of asking the Universe to meet my needs, and had it happen again and again. What I hadn't figured out yet was how not to sabotage the very thing I wanted in the first place. I had railroaded through my life with such irreverent abandon that is really is miraculous in retrospect that I had any semblance of normalcy whatsoever. But I did. I lived a very normal, middle class life with a great stable job full of the necessary benefits. My kids did the normal kid activities and I found myself thrust into the life of a soccer mom. Anamchara lives a very different life by contrast. Not only does he walk a very specific road of spiritual belief, but he's raising his children very differently from the IPod, video game world I had unknowingly allowed my children to slip into. Part of my difficulty with him was in trying to figure out how he would fit into my preconceived notion of the white picket fence, maybe not picket, but into my definition of what I wanted my life with my partner to look like. And then the problem became blaringly apparent. I had no idea what that was. I had built my intention around the sovereign principle of total autonomy. It was me and my kids and my animals, period. I hadn't made any space at all in my life for a real relationship to actually show up. I had sent out the intention to the Universe for my One to show up, but hadn't ever made any room for him to settle in. So to speak, there was no room at the inn.

I began to pray. I began to quietly reflect and in a moment's notice, the road became clear. Forty years of knowing what I thought I wanted disappeared into the falsehoods of the fear that had created it. It became crystallized. I had been so wrong. In those places inside me where I truly believed I wanted complete autonomy got replaced with another truth, one so deep seated and covered in the growth of weeds so dense it took heavy excavation to the truth of my soul to uncover. I wanted something 180 degrees different than I always thought I believed. I wanted it all. I wanted a full partnership, with my equal --building our hopes and dreams together. I mean, every step of the way – a full equal partnership, not one where I do all the work or where I ride on the coat tails of another's passion but one where we come together and share the joy and sorrows of all that life has to offer in every way.

One day I sat down and wrote for myself what I called "My Intentions" and I walked through every step of what I wanted my life to look like. What my relationship would look like, what my career would look like and what my family dynamics would be built upon. When I was done I knew I had uncovered my real truth. Anamchara had opened the door for me to challenge the very foundation of what I believed to be true. I could hide no longer. My soul was clear that it was time to stop lying to myself and own my own divine right to have the things in my life the way I wanted them to be.

Deservingness is a word that would come up in my sessions with my Seer. She would reflect often about my space of "deservingness" being too small. It took me a long time to understand what that meant. There is another crossroads that I think happens frequently on most human journeys, at least it did in mine. It's that space where the Wicked Ego Witch plants her nasty little seeds that whisper, "Do I really deserve what is happening to me in this moment?" It's most relevant to the times when really good things are happening. It happened when I finally owned my dream home. I sabotaged it because I believed I didn't deserve it – just ask the Wicked Ego Witch. She was appalled I had the balls to buy it in the first place.

How many countless relationships had I, either knowingly or not, sabotaged because they held too much promise, were too real? It had happened over and over again. The relationships that had the possibility of being really good I ran from immediately following the epiphany that, "This could be the one." The bad relationships, I held on to for eons longer than human decency should have allowed. The Wicked Ego Witch was all too happy to oblige me and cackle in sinister delight as I clung and acted a fool for the relationships that were just plain wrong.

My relationship with Anamchara was challenging the very foundation of how I behaved, in every way. I was supremely conscious of what I was thinking and what I was doing. What I wasn't ready to do yet was stop the behavior or not have the thoughts happen at all. My journal is full of epiphanies where I say the same thing over and over again. Slow down, stay open, let go and trust the process, come from a place of center and balance, be discerning and objective. Do this differently. Did I? Absolutely not. I hadn't quite gotten to that bend in the River.

I had already come to the place where I knew I did not want to live my life without him. What I could never do is picture what my life would look like with him in it. Our lifeboats in the River of Life were bound together. The connection we had together was still haphazard and ill-defined but we were there, navigating, together. I could never spin a fantasy of the ring, the wedding and the happily ever after that I had built so many relationship possibilities on to this point. Wow.. socialization. As little girls I think we're reared on the fantasy. As much as most of us wouldn't admit it out loud, I think we do have to have some sort of benchmark picture in our heads in order to move forward in a relationship. For me, relationships came with a set of expectations. What they hadn't ever come with was boundaries.

I started to feel like I was giving more in our relationship than I was receiving. While at face value our relationship still felt mutual, I felt like I was leading the way. He would call, sometimes infrequently always claiming chaos or confusion in his life. Anamchara was definitely a very busy man. His schedule could be mind-boggling. But there I was again, making excuses. He'd call, after a few days and lull me into that beautiful space of pure spiritual connection. Our conversations were always deep and introspective. I could say things to him that I never dared to say to anyone else. I could push on him to expand his thinking in ways I wouldn't have dreamed to do with most other people. That type of deeply profound connection was incredibly addictive to me. It was a level and depth of my personality that hadn't ever been encouraged or understood by the men who had come before him. Why would they of? My choices and expectations of those that came before were always from a place of control. And intellectual control was as good as any. I was talking a good game, of being open and unattached to any outcome but that, in retrospect was a line of nonsense and fantasy that I fed myself so I could believe I was playing the game by the rules the Anamchara and I had established early on. Actually, they were the rules he established. He was clear about his need to stay open to whatever came his way. And yes, that meant other women. He set the pace of communication, calling or calling back at his convenience. I made the plans and he chose to accept or decline. What part of any of this was ok? Where were my needs? Where were my boundaries? All I felt was the emotional chaos of tacitly agreeing to play the game of relationship by someone else's rules. I just had to agree on some level so I could pretend to be ok. It is in the pretend part that the Wicked Ego Witch slides her spiked boot into the room and begins to take a foothold.

And we danced...

Dancing is a part of my soul. There is really nothing in the world I love more than the true synchronization of two intimate lovers on the dance floor completely connected and in rhythm. It's a level of connection and energy that is difficult, if not impossible to describe, if you've never experienced it. Anamchara and I often talked of dancing together, but to this point we never had. I think I just got tired of waiting so I baited him, with a one line Facebook post that I was going out. What I didn't expect was the phone to ring during my drive. We had made some tentative plans to spend the weekend together that he cancelled for reasons I knew the minute he spoke them were completely bogus. In a tit-for-tat chess move, I called his bluff and with his phone call he played his check mate. The conversation started about the dance and his wishes that I find the right partner to enjoy the evening. We spoke of the seduction of the tango and the fluidity of other partner dances and then the conversation turned dark.

I could feel his energy shift towards despair as if the talk about dancing had been a clever façade to open the conversation to what he really needed to say. As he continued to talk, a feeling of darkness wound its way through the phone line and up the center of my spine in spasms of madness. There was a dark desperation in his voice as he began to talk about anger, guilt and shame. He was in a very dark place. Reflecting off a headlight in front of me as I drove closer to the bar, I could see her again in my mind's eye, it was Satori, the black mare from his property, the Dark Horse. She stood shivering against the reflection of the rain that was beating down on the hood of my truck. The sense I got in her image was one of defeat and again, of fear. Why was the Dark Horse Satori from his property continuing to show herself to me like a dream? What was she trying to tell me I wondered? These images of her continued to shock and surprise me.

    I was worried about him and as he continued to speak, little edges of panic started to creep up on the back of my neck. He had told me early on in the conversation that he was waiting for a friend to arrive. I felt better when he finally did, and relieved to actually hear his friend's male voice in the background of the conversation. They had planned an evening of male distractions under the guise of a meeting. To say I felt slighted for his cancellation of our weekend for boy games is an understatement.

    As I hung up the phone a thought came to me about the dark place we all find ourselves in occasionally. He was starting to open himself enough to me to share that dark space within. I started calling that place of desperation "dancing with the darkness." It's about being a place of dark emotions and learning to go with their flow. Every journey on the River of Life has those places where we're shrouded in darkness and the eddy is casting us about in the current. The storms of emotion swirl around us as we feel helpless against their power and pull. We all have those places in our River, what we choose to do when we find ourselves there is as personal as is the feelings causing the eddy itself. Anamchara found himself in this place; something had him shrouded in confusion. I had no choice but to let him navigate his lifeboat all by himself as I let go of his dark energy and stepped inside to dance.

    And I danced. I spent the evening fully connected

to the music and the energy that envelops the place I return to when I want a reminder of younger days in my life, days where men were easy and alcohol flowed freely. I don't go for those reasons anymore. I simply go to feel young and beautiful and dance the dances that are such a part of my natural rhythm and body I can do them gracefully and with an ease that requires no effort at all. In the Anamchara's honor, I tried to dance the one dance I could never do very well. Once, years back, I had been trying to do the west coast swing. Probably drunk, I tripped over my partner's feet and fell loudly to the ground. Humiliated, as good dancers are when they make a mistake, I stubbornly refused to dance that dance again until that night. It was a beautiful experience of learning to let go, to leave a past of perfectionism and expectation behind that didn't suit me any longer. It was a beautiful expression of being in the moment and letting things happen and leaving the past where it belonged, behind me.

Pandora's Box....

The next night the phone rang. Anamchara was ready to begin to tell the truth of his dark side. He talked of grieving, he talked of loss. He talked of failed relationships and the women who had come before me, those that he had loved profoundly like his ex-wife, whom he believed he would share a lifetime. While he didn't seem to be stuck in a love gone by, he certainly seemed stuck in failed opportunity and lost dreams. It's a difficult thing to be open and free with a willing heart to risk love again. For as much as my Anamchara radiated love for all things, I believed he stood in fear and confusion about opening his own heart in relationship with another. He talked of relationships where just as he had opened his heart, and began to love again, the other turned tail and ran in the opposite direction. I held my breath hoping that he couldn't see the legacy of the exact same behavior in me.

At the time I thought he trusted me enough to share his most private fears, or perhaps in retrospect it was a dare, "See me for who and what I am," but I doubt it. We had come so far in our ability to be real with each other that he opened his wounds so that I might hold for him the space of compassionate knowing of another. I could empathize because I had traveled the same journey. Failed relationships were the neon t-shirt I wore covered with shame and blame, right along with him. I could absolutely understand the path he had walked to get to this place having walked the same path as well. He finally said, "I could have been with you this weekend, and I was just too confused." He talked about past relationships and the scars they had left behind. I wondered as he talked, about what the impact of losing his normal body functioning had on his self-esteem and fear of loss. What must it be like, to start in this lifetime able bodied, and then have his self perception distorted by the very real life experience of traumatic injury and loss? At face value, he was Superman in my eyes. There was absolutely nothing he could not do. Yes, he did have to do things a bit differently but the end result was powerful and complete. In this entire conversation that circled around lifetimes of loss, he never once mentioned his physical differences. Maybe the scars were still too bright and inflamed in its power in his life to be understood or conscious to him at all. Part of healing and moving on is the ability to identify the damage in the first place. Perhaps I do him no justice at all. Maybe he didn't mention it because he'd already thought it to death. It's hard to say. For as much as I believed I knew and understood the Anamchara, I hadn't even scratched the surface.

Our relationship was extremely physically passionate. It was intense and provocative. We were lovers in every way except one. It's curious to me the difficulty I have today, in writing this tale to admit the entire truth, and that truth is, in my heart we had made love a thousand times. Not one single thing was lacking in our passion. I had never felt so honored, so devoured, so completely loved for every single physical inch of me. But, in the traditional sense of 'having sex' we had not. Nothing about our relationship was traditional or usual for me so really, this aspect shouldn't resonate inside me as such a surprise. It seems to diminish the physical passion we had together up to this point to say it hadn't been completed. What did completed really mean? I was starting to learn about expectations and definitions. Anamchara was trying to learn the same thing.

"I have never wanted anything more than to make love to you. I could literally drag you by your hair and devour you. I can't understand why I stop." He finally said. What was I supposed to say to that? He started talking again about being very worried he was going to break my heart. I guess it wasn't registering, the back story Anamchara was dancing around, to understand where this fear of hurting me was coming from. Maybe I didn't want to know enough to ask directly to get a straight answer.

It is interesting how my intellect and ego could tie this up in a neat little package, complete with a big red bow that I could live with. It was all great right up until the very moment emotion welled up and threatened to engulf the banks of reason. On a rational level, everything he was saying to me during our telephone call made perfect sense. He was scared. He owned that for himself. His life was in chaos. He owned that for himself. He wasn't sure what he was feeling about anything going on in his life, me included. He never changed his story that he just, "Couldn't see where this was going between us, but he was still open to the journey."

We had just scratched the surface of our true depth of humanity with each other, at least Anamchara did. He was bringing his dark side to the table. I wasn't quite ready to do the same. He asked me to bring my truth and vulnerability to our relationship when I was ready, that it was important to him to know the dark side of me as well. The conversation was deep and profound and we went to those places that are difficult, if not impossible to share with another human being whose opinion matters to you. I tried, I really did to make the words of my truth come out through this intense and powerful conversation but I just couldn't do it. Not yet. Intellectually, I was completely supportive. I told him again that I was prepared to handle my own heart. The words I said to him were, "Trust me to know my own heart."

Up until a month before I wasn't sure I had any other type of heart but the muscular one beating in my chest. A month before I was emotionally frozen tundra with no global warming in sight. How in the world could I have possibly rationalized away a man who was being so completely honest by saying, "Hey, I don't know where this is leading, I am all screwed up inside and I am not convinced of who and what you are supposed to be to me." Actually, he never said the convinced part. That's my editorial and subjective license to embellish. But the truth is, that is the truth. He just wasn't convinced. Effortless Grace continued to whisper, "Stay open – let things be what they are." I told him over and over again that I was totally ok just letting things go where they needed to go and that if in fact, he was not the one who was meant to be in a life partnership with me, whom ever was, would be incredible. I assured him that it was the journey that was important, not the outcome. "Liar, liar, pants on fire," screamed the Wicked Ego Witch as my conciliatory words of wisdom and support poured out of me like the plague.

I think he believed that if we "officially" made love (whatever that meant) that things might change or grow deeper for me. Not likely, I was on the fast track to full blown love, without ever being penetrated. I couldn't see how making it official was going to change anything in that regard. But, that was the little girl inside of me talking, the one who believed that sex equaled love. It was the only thing she knew. The adult woman in me hadn't found her voice yet to say, "Wait a minute. What we have is too powerful and too real to be diminished by having it happen too soon and before you are totally sure." I just didn't know any better. It was to be another step on the journey.

I have this habit of showing up to relationships as my most perfect self. How can I be of value to you? How can I make your life easier? I'm not going to bring you all my negative emotional stuff, at least not for awhile anyway. One thing I can say for sure about Anamchara is that he brought himself, his truth, from the very beginning. Me? I brought perfection. I brought happiness and sunshine which is really what I felt, but I saved the dark side for those private moments alone in my shame. In fact, I rarely admitted to even myself I had a dark side at all. I had worked too hard in my life to achieve perfection, whatever that means. It was a fraud, a fallacy. It was the Wicked Ego Witch's lame attempts to try to silence her own voice. I was drowning in my own pretend fantasy of the perfection I thought I'd worked so hard to achieve, the perfection that makes no mistakes, makes all the right choices and always does the right thing. It is the perfection that raises perfect children and has the perfectly kept house -- the perfection that only exists in the fantasy of imagination. Anamchara could see right through it. I think he became uncomfortable in his own real humanity against my façade of perfection. He goaded me to bring my truth, my dark side to the table and I feared against opening Pandora's box.

When you're a seeker on a journey, the lessons unfold at mock speed and that is no joke. It took me less than 24 hours of curiosity at what I might find in the dreaded box to throw it wide open. I begged Anamchara to show up at the table and let me unleash the fury of my pent up emotion and pain. It was almost a dare.

The next day I woke with my own soul truth screaming in my consciousness. It was not ok to make love before both of us could bring our entire beings to the experience full of complete love and commitment. I realized in a moment how afraid I was to be vulnerable. I didn't trust him to honor my dark side, the one that was beginning to burst through the surface of perfection I forced myself to believe was true. When the box came flying open I unleashed a fury of unexpressed emotion and Anamchara was nowhere to be found.

The Witch descended from the darkness in a rush of smoky fog, the air unrelenting in its thick despair. Her black magic cast widely about her as I lay helpless in my surrender to her litany of my legacy of shame and misery for a life yet unlived. Jagged black torrents of hopelessness came in wave after wave as an assault on my emotions. Each crashed through me in a rage of feeling that shattered me to the core of my humanity. In the depth of my despair she reached for me with her talons of power and I let her. I let the barrage of historical failure and self-depreciation come to the surface to be acknowledged. The Wicked Ego Witch in her resplendent, misogynistic misery was primed to declare her epic victory as I lay spent and helpless to stop her.

In my emotional fugue I did the only thing I knew how to do. I prayed, and I mean seriously, albeit perhaps desperately, prayed, "Heavenly Father, I come to you in humility and gratitude asking for redemption in your light. Please give me the strength to stand in the middle of this battle with myself. Please give me the strength to see my Truth." Just as the words slipped through my shallow breath and took flight, a window to my truth opened. I saw the continuum of pain I had woven throughout my life. When the rainbow of my Truth opened, I began to cry in torrents of healing water that contained the seeds of my enlightenment. I cried for the little girl who gave far too much of herself, far too often. I cried for the years

I spent in desperation waiting for a man to come to rescue me. I cried for the woman, so broken, so full of bitterness and regret that I had become. I saw my own vicious hatred of myself and all the choices I'd made throughout my life to confirm what I believed to be true. I had become the blind servant to a calculated and cruel mistress, The Witch. And for the first time in my life I could see her standing in front of me, dark and translucent, a simple figment of the strength of my imagination that had created her. In that realization she lost power and her fury raged uncontained. In an equal and magnanimous fury, Radical Faith appeared whole and radiant beside me. Gently moving me to the side, she rallied her battle cry of forgiveness. Her sword glimmered in radiance of Hope and Truth as it circled The Witch for war. As the auburn haired beauty exhaled in readiness, something in me released. As I watched them battle, something in me gave way. When the golden loving arms of Effortless Grace surrounded me, sheltered and protected behind her shield, I cried. As the tears fell I was surrounded in the golden light of forgiveness, compassion and grace. I could feel, from the center of my being, forgiveness for all the transgressions I had committed to myself. For all the transgressions I allowed from others. I looked at myself with the new found eyes of compassion and wisdom for the journey that had brought me to this place. In this realization of self-love I could breathe with an expansiveness I had never known before. As I stood in the golden light of my own true grace I could see my own humility and humanity. Pandora's box was finally empty.

I am so glad Anamchara didn't show up as I was railing through unexpressed emotion and grief for the unconscious life I had been living. I am truly grateful that I was given the Effortless Grace to move through that experience all on my own. There were moments I thought I would literally drown in my own sea of hatred and despair. And there were moments of profound grace when

I could see the absolution contained in my own Divine truth. The perfection that simply is: whoever and whatever I am, in every single moment of my life.

When he finally called I tried to tell him what I'd been through but I couldn't find words to describe the power, fury and ultimate healing of the waterfall behind me. I did try to explain to him how really afraid I had been to open up to the emotions I was feeling inside. I guess that's what happens when the storm has passed and my mind could exercise some intellectual control over what I said out loud. I started to realize I didn't know myself at all, and that I didn't trust what I did know. I started seeing the self-brutalization I had been showering on myself and in my life so unconsciously. It was interesting to me to be able to stand back from my body, ego or personality, whatever word made most sense in that moment, to be able to see myself from a place of neutrality. It's only in being able to see, and identify that the winding bend of the River starts to come into view.

The Roar of the Ocean...

Anamchara had often talked about a fantasy of taking me to a secluded beach house for a weekend and getting lost with me in the sand. He described with words brimming in passion and possibility cooking meals together, listening to music and just being completely engulfed with me in every way.

Our relationship to this point had been extremely private. He hadn't been included in my life, except for his brief trip to take me to the hospital for my angiogram. He had met my children, but in a very controlled, short lived manner and my kids didn't know anything other than that he was a friend who was taking me to the hospital. It is such a tricky dance when children are a part of the potential of the relationship. As a single mother I believe very strongly that I don't want my children to suffer a revolving door of men. The majority of men I had dated before the Anamchara had long been family friends or had not been introduced to my children until the relationship was well established. Even then, it was critically important to me that my children see my partner as a family friend.

He was just as protective about the people in his life as I was. I had not been exposed really to anyone except for a couple of close friends on my trips to his house and I hadn't been introduced to his children. Our relationship lived in our private world of togetherness, and in truth, I really didn't want it any other way. Our relationship, at least for me, was fast approaching something very significant. It felt like time to share him with the important people in my world.

In casual passing one day I mentioned that my family was heading to the beach for the weekend. I asked him if he was interested in joining us. Surprising me, he said yes. I think his agreement was, in part, due to the fact that I had strategically and selfishly planned for us spend the first night together and alone without the rest of my family. It had been a few weeks since we'd been together, and the time had come to share our space again.

The universe has funny little ways of answering our questions when we ask them, if only we are paying attention. As I was driving to the beach, I started thinking and worrying about him, wondering what kind of energy and emotional space he might be in when I found him again. He'd had another rough week and the last time I spoke to him, he seemed scattered and distant. Just as the worry crept up along the edges of my consciousness I looked up, and there immediately next to me was a sign that said, "His name, and the words OK Market." I roared with laughter. The universe was sending me a message that he was OK. It was the funniest, oddest coincidence I had ever seen. Why in the world would someone name their market, in a little remote highway town someone's name and then add OK Market had me in fits of universal giggles. I learned in that moment, that humor and grace really does exist all around me. I really wished I would have had a camera with me because it was one of those times when the Universe's response was so swift and so clear all I could to do was grin in understanding and amusement.

When I arrived at the hotel, I walked in to get our room thinking I'd have at least an hour or so to get ready for his arrival. As I walked back out to my car I pulled up short looking at an attractive man sitting in his car. I was completely caught off guard that the man in the car was Anamchara. He had arrived much earlier than expected. Given his propensity for being late and being lost, it was a beautiful and unexpected surprise. Our weekend was about to unfold.

There is something mystical and reverent for me about being on the coast. Staring out across the expanse of the water and out onto the horizon always makes me think about Creation. For me, the ocean calls to untold magic and the energy of the expanse of possibility. I feel the same way when I gaze on rugged peaks and valleys of the mountains. While I am not particularly religious in nature, my very essence is one of reverent spirituality. I understand the scientific explanations of how our home world came to be but the dry scientific explanation seems shortsighted and limited in its view when I look towards great natural beauty of extraordinary proportion. I stand strong in my belief that something much larger than ourselves is responsible for its creation.

The Oregon coast is unlike any I've ever experienced. The ruggedness of the rocky coast line is scattered with driftwood, sand dunes and miles of unending beach that have been spared the intrusion of humanity with our usual attempts to blend into its spectacular natural essence. Civilization has been asked to keep its artificial dwellings off the main shore line in most areas in part due to progressive legislature of politics before its time. The beaches are nothing short of spectacular. It's wild and untamed, at least most of it. And generally speaking, the weather defends its reputation. Usually windy, and very cold, we were subjects of a rare winter treat, a simply a spectacular day. Our day was nothing short of incredible. The sun was radiant in the sky and there wasn't one single gust of wind to make it even remotely chilly. It was a grand opening that whispered the beauty and surprise of what I hoped was to come. It took only seconds inside our hotel room to be passionately consumed with each other. Somewhere deep inside I could feel the Universe smile in contentment at our union.

In his normal life, Anamchara runs around mach ten with his hair on fire living each and every moment caught up in to-do lists and schedules. Building new programs, facilitating groups and working with his horses takes up every spare moment he has. It's the world we're living in. So much to do, so many things to accomplish, it wasn't his nature to take much down time to relax. Every time we came together, it would take him a long while to unwind. When he agreed to take this weekend trip away from his world with me he made one thing very clear. He didn't want to talk, he simply just wanted to Be.

My Anamchara is a grown up, very strong little boy in his heart of hearts. He loves to be naughty and play rambunctiously. I don't think he has any idea of how incredibly strong he is physically. He is a true physical force which one might think is odd given that he has very little use of his left side. The strength and flexibility on the right side, along with a lifetime of adaption has created a man capable of most any physical feat. He is not a large man by any means. At face value, he shouldn't possess a tenth of the strength that he does. But he does. And some of my very favorite times were when his little boy came out to play.

One of the beautiful life lessons I learned in my relationship with Anamchara was about the sides we carry with us as adults. We shared a great many conversations about the reverent spirituality contained in Native American teachings. Described in some beliefs is the nature of how each of us learns to navigate the four sides we carry within us to create harmony and balance. When one of the sides falls out of balance with the other sides, we begin to face life challenges. We each have a little boy and little girl in us, and we have an adult man and woman within us as the teaching explains. They each have different perceptions, strengths and challenges. This view of the world and concept of personal balance brought me a great deal of insight into who I was and how I was walking through my world. My adult male is very loud, and very in control most of the time. He's probably very closely related to my Wicked Ego Witch. He is commanding in his presence and can be punitive and cruel in his remarks inside my head. He is also the side of me that has the incredible strength and stamina that has pushed me to accomplish several acts of great courage and brilliance. My woman is very compassionate and loving but struggles with trust and boundaries. She is the side of me that is nurturing and protective of everything she allows herself to love. She is the side of me that shrinks in fear and indecisiveness. My little girl is sparkly, mischievous and full of fun. She's also precocious and spoiled. She is the side of me who acts impulsively and doesn't stop or think of consequences at all. She's also holds the side of me that believes in miracles and can walk out on pure faith in the goodness of life. The little boy in me is the one I have the hardest time learning to honor and encourage. As I've aged I've lost appreciation for the gifts that he could bring. When I was younger he was the side of me that was adventurous and spontaneous and carried a fearless wonder about the world.

As I started to pay attention to these teachings, I started asking myself "Who is in control here, which side is asking to be heard?" If I was facing a challenging situation, I'd think about which side of me was speaking the loudest, and try to see the situation from my other sides. I believe we forget that lingering inside each of us that is the child we used to be. That child lives on, in some of us very unconsciously. Our "little ones" as I call them, can destroy lives with their impulsive, unconscious flights of fancy. My little girl can drain my bank account in a moment's notice on a shopping spree. She can throw a temper tantrum to rival a world war. In a flight of insecurity and impetuousness, she can sabotage my greatest efforts to accomplish my hopes and dreams.

Our "little ones" if allowed to play and express their childish desires in healthy ways can bring un-measureable happiness and well rounded experiences to our adulthoods. Their gifts to us should be honored and encouraged, not grounded and sent to their rooms. Anamchara understands this and when his little boy and my little girl came out to play – they were the very best of friends.

We let our little ones run free on the beach that day, and it's one of the greatest experiences I've ever had of being truly in the moment and allowing my little girl full reign. We ran, we played, we laughed and we danced – right into the surf. In a mind bending burst of energy and pure physical power the little boy inside the Anamchara wanted to wrestle. He caught me sideways and down I went, right into the freezing winter shoreline. In a most chivalrous gesture, he came right down into the surf with me. Lying on our backs, laughing hysterically, I felt a freedom and lightness of being that shimmered to my very essence. It was a magical feeling of pure childish pleasure.

That is the part of my inner child that seeks to come to the surface, the part of me who wants to be completely free. It is the part of me that I seek to relegate to the farthest reaches of my consciousness. Once I'd experienced the beautiful side of my little girl, I was able to see her for her precocious beauty and inner spark of pure goodness and radiant light that was inside of me all along. I make great efforts today to honor and welcome my little girl when she decides she wants to act mischievously. Interestingly enough, when this side of me is honored, she stops her temper tantrums of childish impetuousness and I seldom find myself in the mall.

Soaking wet from the surf, we began to walk. Along the way I started taking pictures. I took one picture that still to this day is my very favorite picture of me, of all time. It's not that I look spectacular or thin or even particularly interesting. It's the simple look of pure, radiant joy shining from every cell of my face. It's a simple picture, the kind you take of two people holding the camera just far enough out of frame to catch both faces. The smile on his face is pure radiance as well. You can see our very souls in this picture – and our little children wide eyed and deliriously happy for being allowed to play.

We were allowed the rare privilege of a coastal sunset on our night together at the beach. I will always think of that as a Universal blessing of what was to come. I've always known, from the very beginning that we have shared lifetimes together, before. I can't explain the knowing, it simply just is. It's the kind of visceral knowledge that can't be explained with words. I'd never really given past lives much thought in all honesty before my time with Anamchara. In theory and at face value, it just made sense to me but with him, the intensity, knowledge and complete knowing was so real and so thorough, no other explanation seemed to make any sense. Between us, we shared a living déjà vu. We'd been here and done this before. I'd feel glimpses of things I knew we had done before but I had no knowledge of having shared it with him in this lifetime. Fairly early on in our relationship I started noticing that we shared an ability with each other, the same kind of ability that I believe every human has the ability to do, but just have no understanding that it exists or how to actually do it. We can call to each other, and always get an energetic response. I can literally close my eyes and focus in on him and be able to feel exactly where he is and what he's feeling. It doesn't always work that clearly, so it was easy in the beginning to believe myself spinning wild fantasies. But over time, I began to trust my intuitive energetic responses from this man.

Energy exists all around us. We are made of energy. Our very essence is pure power and energetic charge. If you think of an electric spark being able to jump across power lines, you can begin to picture how energy shift between two people happens. Much is being written and talked about in this regard. Most people, living unconsciously and in fear dismiss the idea of telepathy, energy exchange and intuitive insight. Energy attracts like energy. Human beings are so tactile and scientific, that we have a really hard time trusting in anything we can't rationalize or scientifically explain.

I could understand the written pages in the books I'd read that talked about the energetic, telepathic and intuitive connection between people. Intellectually I could get it, it made sense. But I hadn't ever experienced it. When I did, it was easy to dismiss as a flight of fantasy or imagination, and I'd always been very imaginative. I'd always been very consciously aware of our ability as humans to energetically connect with people just like us, to re-create patterns. Take the abused woman, who leaves her abuser only to be caught in another abusive situation that follows. This woman carries the emotional energy of a victim, and an abuser can energetically spot it coming from a million miles away. Its only when the abused changes her very energy signature, from doing a lot of really hard emotional work, that the energy signature changes and she stops attracting the same kind of man.

Anamchara and I share this kind of energy signature with each other. We can feel each other from a million miles away. I feel very fortunate that somewhere, albeit unconsciously, I had changed my energy resonance to attract another amazingly good human being. It is part of how I know I'm evolving as a spiritual being, the kind of people that are showing up in my life are completely different. They carry the energy of passion and love. It's the energy I was finally stepping into, and owning for myself.

As night fell, the obvious sexual tension between us built to its crescendo. In a rare burst of spoken insight Anamchara said to me, "I know why it seems so hard to me to make love to you, you are just too important to me." In that moment, the earth stood still. I had waited my entire life for the one man who would wait for me. In an almost unintelligible whisper I answered, "I've never been important enough for anyone to wait." I knew in that moment that I was in love with my Anamchara. I knew that I could make love to him from a place of pure truth and honor my needs as a woman, finally and for the very first time in my life. As we made love I felt a warmth and tenderness I had never experienced before him. I felt washes of grief, sadness and regret as well, and that caught me by surprise. It was a night filled with beginnings and endings as he compassionately surrounded me as I moved through the emotions that tumbled uncontrollably to the surface of my life to be released in the Rivers flow. I could feel myself tossing away in the current the pattern of the self-defeating belief that sex equaled love. Finally all the destructive ranting of the Wicked Ego Witch around this life-long issue, were laid to rest. I knew as our passionate sexual tide ebbed and flowed, that I would never give my power away as a woman, to a man who didn't honor, respect and love me completely, again. While the beauty of our union was overwhelming and complete, the healing came in the Knowing. What I knew now, through the eyes and love of my Anamchara was that I was whole and complete and worthy of real love. As the dawn rose in red-gold waves of majesty across the horizon I quietly slipped out of our bed. Something profound and powerful had happened to me the night before, in the arms of this soul friend I had found myself; a powerfully beautiful, totally complete woman.

Watching him stir quietly under the covers I began to think about what the day ahead would bring us. It was time to open the door to family. I was going to introduce this man, who had become so important to me to the people who knew me best in the world. Could they see the difference in me? Could they see the changes I felt so deeply? I honestly, to this day don't know the answer.

Watching Anamchara navigate the early beginnings of a relationship with my children became a lesson to me in how to relate to the world. At first hello he was down on his knees, eye to eye with each of my children with warm greeting and allowed them the natural curiosity and questions any child would have of a man who walks through this world with a physical body that looks so different from theirs. No question was out of line, no amount of intense gazing mattered. He stayed on his knees, in that space with my children quietly and reverently honoring each of them with his fullest of attention. In the flick of a switch my children were enamored. In that moment I learned about being human, about showing the world your humanity, the very real essence that you are. I watched a man so full of life reach my children by simply being present enough to acknowledge their very simple child-like curiosity. When as an adult did I learn to hide my truth?

We spent time at the aquarium watching the beautiful grace of the jelly fish in their ethereal flight through the salt water. We touched sea-rays and held anemones and talked about the mysteries contained in the sea. I found myself alive and curious as well, taking the time and patience to allow my children to foster their own curiosity about a world so different from their own. I followed Anamchara's example, and shown in its beautiful light. We laughed together and I had moments of quiet delight in watching my oftentimes shy daughter laughing in the arms of this man I had come to love. It was a glimpse of family, the kind of family I'd been unable to create on my own. My Wicked Ego Witch and the puffed up, overbearing control of my man side that could never believe I'd find the courage or conviction to share what I'd created with another, stood watching quietly.

As day stretched into evening, Anamchara and I were left alone in the beach house we'd rented, with all of the kids in my family. My niece and nephew were with us and the little boy in the Anamchara came back out to play. Raucous pillow fights ensued as the teenage kids were awed by his strength and flexibility. It was loud, it was energetic and the kids engaged and played just as hard as Anamchara. Eventually we began to quiet down. As the fireplace crackled and burned, it was time to turn to storytelling. Anamchara is a magic man of storytelling and of connecting with kids. It is his mission, his passion. It is his life.

I have never experienced such power and hold over a group of children. As the drum began to play its melody, Anamchara began to speak. He spoke of tradition, he spoke of roles and responsibilities, he spoke of personal power and the truth of what it means to be a spiritual being regardless of age. He saw these kids, saw their truth and he spoke it out loud. I watched with intense interest in the looks on the faces of the children I loved so much. These were my children, my family, and I was watching them be acknowledged and validated in ways that we don't normally do in our fast paced American culture. I've never seen such concentration, such attention in my children before. We sang Native American songs of tradition, songs that call out our very human essence. One of the songs was the warrior song. In this song, each person in the circle was asked sing their warrior. Anamchara chose me first to lead the ceremony in which we were all to partake.

When the drumming turned its attention to me, I literally froze solid and couldn't open my vocal chords. I simply couldn't find my voice. Besides the fact that one of my greatest fears is singing in front of other people, I just couldn't make the vocalizations happen. I was sitting in a room full of all the people I loved, most of whom were children and I couldn't sing the warrior song. It was in that moment when I realized I had lost my voice. I had lost my ability to speak my truth from the center of my divinity. Anamchara wouldn't let me off the hook. He held my space intent with his eyes, patiently and with love until I could find the courage and the resolve to sing. While no one likely noticed, perhaps except for Anamchara, my energy shifted. I felt deflated and humiliated. I had let myself down in my own knowing. Not because I couldn't sing, but because I knew I had lost my power, my truth, my voice. I realized that the Warrior spirit I had always carried inside me had lost the way.

The evening came to a close, the ceremony of drumming, story-telling and song was lived and received. Each one of the children got up and went quietly without complaint to bed. I was in awe. I had never witnessed such complete and truthful presence of an adult with a group of children. He looked deep into the hearts and minds of my children and in doing so, validated their very worth and honor as a human beings. I'd never seen such validation of spiritual truth in the eyes of a child. Each child went to bed that night feeling seen and heard in the Universal sense. I had intellectually known about the Anamchara's gifts, but on this night I had the extreme honor of being present and included in his life work. I was humbled and grateful that my children, even if for only one small moment in time, were able to experience such profound truthful sight of their very essence. For this gift, I will always be eternally grateful.

I had hurt my back earlier in our day trying to lift an ice cooler out of my truck, and had spent most of the day trying to avoid doing any more damage. It was amusing to watch this powerful man carry around my purse as we made our way through our adventures of the day. As we went to bed, Anamchara offered me a gift of passion and attention that I couldn't refuse. Afraid to move much, he offered me exquisite physical respite from my aching back. He loved me with so much attention that the memory still burns brightly in my soul. It was the touch of a lover, of a soul mate. It was the physical recognition of our connection to each other, the one that never needs any words or explanation. It was the kind of loving that glows in the beauty and quiet recesses of lifetimes.

Our weekend had come to an end. It was time to say goodbye to Anamchara. Our parting always left me empty and spent. Being that absorbed with another takes a good deal of energy and effort. While I wouldn't have traded or changed any single moment we ever spent together, the exhaustion of trying to live every single drop of every single moment together would take its toll. It would usually take me a few days to shake off the lingering energy he would always leave behind. I think I'd make it last on purpose, just to keep him close to me.

After a lifetime of failed relationships I became very conscious of my attempts to live this relationship with Anamchara differently. What became really obvious to me was that I had no roadmap for changing my own very relationship nature. It always seemed to me that he could slip so easily back into his life. Perhaps he'd mastered the art of being present in every single moment of his life, and his attention and effort he held with me was just the way he lived every moment. It was a new way of living for me. I could do it, for periods of time, but then I would end up feeling isolated, empty and alone. Perhaps I was giving too much of myself again. Perhaps I was living only for the experiences I shared with this man. It was a pattern I'd re-created in every significant relationship I'd ever had. The only difference this time was I was finally getting conscious of it.

It used to confound me that Anamchara and I would spend so much energy and effort together and then he'd just disappear. Sometimes it would be days before he'd call again. He was pretty good about dropping me an email but after such passionate intensity, I would feel like I'd been marooned on a deserted island. I'd start to spin and the Wicked Ego Witch would start her nasty diatribe of hatred and venom. She'd toss little innuendos deep into my thoughts about other women, about not being good enough to keep him and that he was just like all the others before unworthy of my time and attention. And then the little girl in me would start to whine and tantrum. She is a child of action – she doesn't like to be ignored. My private torture would rage in my mind in the moments between phone calls or weekends. The torture would ravish me for hours on end to the point I'd get so frustrated I'd just be ready to call the whole thing quits. Hell, it was going to end anyway, why not just get it over. And so the tape loops would play, endlessly it seemed. The quiet voice of Radical Faith inside me always spoke the same message, "Stay open…believe."

Manifestation…

There is at least one fact about me that the Wicked Ego Witch doesn't even try to argue about. When I am standing in my own power and passion, I can be a force of nature. I've always known this about myself. I can be focused to the extreme and produce works of great brilliance with very little time and effort. It's a gift, just one of those things about me that I take for granted, but it is another gift that got lost somewhere along the way. As a child I was always passionately deep in one project or another, and as a social justice kind of person it was usually about giving something back to the world. That part of me is just simply how I express myself. What I have never done well is nurture, nurture a passion or a project. That was not my way. I would jump 100% into the deep end, or not even bother to get started at all. The trouble with jumping into the deep end was often I'd misjudge the temperature of the water, catch a glimpse of the danger trolling beneath the surface or feel the pull of the riptide threatening to sweep me away. I'd get scared of the danger, or panic in the riptide and without any tenacity or faith get right back out of the water when the first sign of trouble or difficulty showed up. I am the Queen Mother of chucking it all and finding something new to distract my very active mind. I am learning to ride the ebb and flow of creation. I am learning to nurture and to stay focused. It's part of my journey. The next adventure with Anamchara would begin to lead the way.

 I had begun to feel a shift starting to happen in our relationship just before our trip to the beach. It started shortly after the night I went dancing. It felt like something inside Anamchara had changed and was moving closer to me after the night he began to open his dark side of emotion. It felt like the beginnings of trust. He started engaging more and often, he'd call every day or at least every other. We were connected, we were together. It felt like a partnership was beginning to settle into its foundation for not only me, but for him as well. He would often call and say, "You are the only person in the world I want to talk to." This would follow a horrible day where he just wanted to disappear from the sight of any other human or at least that's what he'd tell me. The center of my very being would sigh softly and begin to settle into the truth that perhaps, finally, I had found my one who was never going to leave.

 I was very involved in Anamchara's life to the extent I became a sounding board and advice maiden as he worked through some of his business related issues. Let's be clear, he didn't call and beg me for my help or opinions. I offered them, freely and likely very insistently. Part of my relationship modus operandi was to make myself invaluable to my partner. That's how I gained my strength and felt the most secure. It's not to say that he needed my help, or even asked for it. He didn't. But we built the beginnings of a partnership that could have easily translated over to a working relationship as well. We trust each other, and that extends to every area of our lives. Anamchara listened when I spoke. He still does.

His life calling resonated with me on just about every level. I believed with my entire being in the power of creating partnerships between horses and people. I was living a personal journey of this Truth in my own life, with my own horse. I couldn't dismiss its inherent ability to create life changing experiences with humans. Humans need experiential feedback that happens in the moment to be able to identify life patterns. Fear is a four-letter word directly connected to safety when navigating a relationship with a 1200 pound creature with its own instinct and intelligence. Learning to trust my own abilities and instincts is a continuing evolution. Having the experiences of facing my fears, and pushing through them were just beginning to build a level of self-confidence that I could take to the rest of my world. His work created an environment that simulates team work, clear intention and the modulation of energy, or, the signals our body language sends to the people in our world. He was working magic by teaching Native American hoop teachings, or the balance of the four directions --body, mind, heart and spirit-- in combination with communication with these incredible four legged partners. His ultimate life dream was to create a sacred land space that was open to all spiritual practices where humans could experience the wisdom of nature and the animals who call our planet home.

Anamchara was struggling, his property was creatively financed and he needed many more physical structures on his land to be able to more comfortably refinance. I had just been through such a similar ordeal with my Ranch, that I understood the emotions and chaos completely. Programs of this nature are hard to finance, often exclusively looking to private donors or grant funding to stay afloat. To this point, Anamchara had invested his whole life savings into making his vision a reality.

I was sitting in a work related meeting just a couple days after our return from the beach trip. Normally zoned out, a little flicker of "pay attention now" shot across my consciousness as an associate began to talk about a new summer project. I felt a jolt of lightening strike. I asked a bunch of questions and realized this same summer program could be designed and built to help Anamchara in his business.

I found it, that zap of pure power and passionate creation come flying to my surface. I became consumed in figuring out how to make this new grant program work for Anamchara. My mind blazed with creative insights and the magician inside me took over. Within three hours, I created a brilliant brainstorm of program design that could have made a huge difference on a whole lot of levels for Anamchara and his life work. I called him immediately and said, "Whatever you're doing, you have to stop and listen to me right now.. I don't care if you choose to do this or not, but I have to tell you, my passion is on fire and it feels amazing." That beautiful side of me, that I love so much had finally come awake. It was spirit driven, it was inspired and I radiated confidence and excitement with every cell in my body. It had been decades since I had felt that type of wake up call to my passionate space of creation. Unfortunately, the cut-off date for project proposals was in ten days. If Anamchara was going to say yes, it was going to take every bit of our combined efforts to get it accomplished in time. He said yes, and the journey to relationship space of creation and partnership opened up.

I offered to go down to his house for the weekend to work on the project. In truth, we couldn't have accomplished the project if we hadn't been together but for me, it was simply and excuse to be able to spend more time in his space. While I was very aware of what he was trying to accomplish, we'd never sat together and discussed the minutia of what he was building. I didn't understand all the parts and pieces, and when I am passionate about something, the parts and pieces have to make sense. I needed him to come out of vision, and into project planning reality and I needed him to do so in a way that I could wrap my brain around it. He is definitely a dreamer. That is part of what I love so much about him. He is a vision carrier, but the practicality of making dreams come true involve the tangible details of a plan. Planning, at least in my perspective, isn't necessarily Anamchara's strength, but it is however, one of mine.

On the drive down for the weekend I was surprised at how nervous and confused I was. I moved into a mode of panic worrying about whether I was going to actually be able to perform at the level of capability and commitment it would take to see this project through. It was performance anxiety, and I hadn't felt it in so long it was disconcerting. Things usually come very easy to me, and they usually come easily with minimal effort. Somewhere on the drive it occurred to me how I have short changed my own 'showing up in the world' by always giving minimal effort. When you have spirit given gifts, they should be given with the full weight of their promise. Maybe that's why internally I always felt like such a fraud. Because I know I am capable of being so much more than I show the world. I am afraid of standing in my own brilliance. I was afraid that I would show up so powerfully during my time with Anamchara that he wouldn't be able to handle it. I've been called intimidating before. I made a decision on that drive, to bring everything I had – not just for him and the project, but for me, to be reminded of the powerful being that I am.

Marianne Williamson wrote a poem about the deepest fear of humans, the fear that we are powerful beyond measure. Somewhere in our journey, Anamchara and I had realized this was a favorite quote that we shared. We talked about the fear of truly stepping in and saying yes to your own power. Why do we do that? Why would I be afraid to be all that I am? I still don't have a good answer but, I'm working on it. Telling this story is a part of that journey.

Satori, the Dark Horse was standing quietly next to the gate alongside the drive as I pulled down the gravel road to his property. I stopped my car and walked over to where she stood alone. Something inside me was powerfully drawn to the Dark Horse, as if I understood her very essence. The closer I got, the more animated her gestures became. She began to paw the ground as her tail wove wildly in the air. It was as if she sensed some excitement, a break-through of sorts. She turned to go away from where I stood at the gate but stopped after only taking a few steps. She arched around, and waved in my direction with her neck as if wondering why I wasn't following. Hesitantly I opened the gate, expecting that she would race off. She'd never allowed me to be so close to her before. My gestures were slow and intentional as I walked through. She took a few more steps forward and stopped again, this time swinging her whole body around to face me. At that moment, the sun burst through an opening in the clouds and together, this dark horse and I were bathed in the light of the heavens that shone down upon us. Cautiously I extended my hand, to reach up just by her shoulder. Her long dark mane gently brushed over my fingers as she closed the gap of the space that was between us. She sighed. And in that moment, I could sigh too. Our body energy was connected to each other by the touch of my hand upon her withers. In the warmth of the sun we stood together quietly. Inside I could feel the beating of my heart in synchronicity with hers. Her whinny broke through the reverie I felt standing so close and connected to her. The sound of her hooves pounding away from where we stood together was a deafening blow to my senses. Once again, I was alone.

When I pulled up to the barn I saw Anamchara waiting with two of his horses, saddled and ready to take us on the journey ahead. For as much as I love horses and for the all time we had spent together, it was surprising to me that we had never taken the journey around his property on horseback. I had been very insistent with him that before we could start to work on the project I needed to tour around his property so that he could show me his vision pace by pace. I guess it made sense to do that with his horse partners who are so much a part of the work that is done there. What I needed was to understand what he saw and where he saw it so I could begin to figure out the logistics of the program design I had come up with. I changed my clothes, still incredibly fearful of riding a horse I didn't know. I had come a long way with my mare Dixie. We'd come to the place where I trusted her not to intentionally endanger me, but every time I was ready to ride her I'd have to very consciously work with my fear pictures to climb on.

Just as I was about ready to mount a beautiful sorrel gelding, Satori ran down the pasture fence line whinnying and shrieking causing horses and humans alike to turn and watch her in surprise. Anamchara said, "Wow, she never acts like that. Generally, she won't come down here until she knows its feeding time. I wonder what has her all worked up?" In the desert, you learn to trust the instincts of your animal partners. Instinctually they can sense danger long before it ever comes into human focus. It's foolish not to pay attention when a horse acts out of character. I finally told him what happened at the gate with Satori when I had pulled into his drive. Shock registered across his face as he said, "She doesn't ever let anyone get that close to her." Something moved powerfully inside me, like something dark was trying to find its way to the light. Hearing the words come out of my mouth was likely more shocking to me than to him. I said, "I think she's asking me not to leave without her, to ride her." "You can't be serious," he answered. Still reeling from my own surprise I answered softly, "Its' ok. We'll be fine." Anamchara opened the corral gate and let the Dark Horse into the barn. She stood quietly while being saddled and seemed to sigh again, as if some healing had happened for her as well. When I lifted my foot to climb into the stirrup I felt my own fear quietly slip out of my body and drift away on the light breeze that was blowing across the desert sky. A sense of peace and confidence flooded my senses as just off in the distance, standing under the shade of a juniper tree I could see them in the radiant sunlight, Radical Faith, with her sword tucked away in its scabbard and Effortless Grace, with her shield slung low across her back. They smiled in acknowledgement for the road I had traveled to be in this place and disappeared.

We moved our horses off slowly as we wound our way around quietly to the places on the property that Anamchara felt were sacred. "This land has its own calling, its own energy. I've had profoundly spiritual moments praying or working in some of these places." He talked about his vision, of creating ecologically and environmentally sound buildings that could be used for a variety of activities. He spoke of partnerships where other organizations could come to this place to do their work. He was trying to build a utopia of learning where kids could be immersed with animals and the natural desert surroundings that filled the field of vision for as far as my eye could see. Finally, we reached the top of a plateau where the junipers became dense. I could sense a change in the energy around me. Anamchara asked me to climb down off of Satori and walk a bit further. We came to a clearing between the junipers and on the ground I could see a circle made of ribbons tied to a red string. It was clear to me that this was his place of spiritual connection, of his vision quest. On the ground were objects that radiated significance. A small wooden house that looked like a toy, a gold ring, shaped in a perfect circle and pieces of brightly colored cloth. He saw me eyeing intently the items that had been placed in an order that appeared significant. "This is where I chose to do my last vision quest. It was a time of asking Spirit to help me let go of the past." In the distance, I heard Satori nicker in response. He continued, "I am so proud of you, I know how hard it was for you to trust Satori. You honored yourself, and her, by facing your fears with courage. I respect that so much about you. I just want you to know how much I appreciate you coming down, taking the time away from your children to help me with this project. I don't know where it will end up, but I'm glad we get the chance to do this together." His body language became very quiet as a peaceful serenity filled the vision quest space that we shared.

I was acutely aware of myself and where my body was in physical relation to his sacred circle. I knew nothing about the sacred tradition of vision quest but was paralyzed in my fear that I was going to do something that might be considered an offense. Then, he invited me inside. "When you enter the sacred circle you can choose to do it one of two ways. You can stomp your foot three times and enter or you can turn your whole body around clockwise, and then enter. You chose what way feels right to you." I hesitated, always so unsure of my own instincts in unfamiliar situations. I thought about stomping my foot, but it seemed frivolous to me so I closed my eyes, tried to find a place of reverence and purpose inside me, circled my body and gently crossed into his vision quest space.

We sat in the middle of his circle with our knees gently touching. He talked about the time he had spent in this place during vision quest and some of the things that had happened for him there. I felt such honor and reverence at being allowed to enter this space with him. I tried to absorb everything that was around me. I focused on the feel of sand beneath my hands as I gently scooped up its warmth, allowing it to run through my fingers. I tried to quiet my mind enough to hear the gentle breeze that was blowing through the branches of the trees that surrounded and seemed to protect us. We had taken this horseback journey, to this place for a reason. It was time to come together, in reverence and prayer and ask that our work together be blessed and productive.

One of the things I had learned so clearly from my experiences with my Ranch, was the strength and power of clear intention, of asking the Universe for exactly what you need and then getting quiet enough to hear the answer. I had hoped when we entered the vision quest circle, to be strong enough to encourage Anamchara through some visioning exercises to help him get clarity on his intentions for this project but for some reason, I still couldn't find my voice, it wasn't my day to step into the role of teacher. Anamchara is a very spiritual man with very clear spiritual practices. I love being around him when he engaged in his rituals of practice. In truth I think it's he who intimidates me in this regard. I felt a deferral of my spiritual truth and knowing to his practices as the prayer continued. He offered me the chance to speak or to pray if I chose, and while I did offer some words in ceremony, I felt very meek and intimidated. When had that happened?

It was another lesson on the journey. I saw all the times I had silenced my own truth in deference. I saw all the times when I silenced my own inner truth to mirror that of another – I was doing it in so many ways, not just in relationships but in work, with friends and with my children. I saw all the times when I was too afraid to try something new, afraid I would look foolish. When had I abandoned my own inner child who wants to explore and learn new things? When had I become so rigid and afraid?

We left the circle and mounted our horses, who had

been quietly waiting in the distance. It was time for us to leave vision and move into the space of creating possibility. Satori, the dark and unpredictable mare was as docile and dependable as the most experienced of ranch mounts for our entire journey of the property. As we returned to the barn, she looked deep into my eyes as a sense of awe and wonder filled the pit of my soul. I had connected with this dark horse and allowed her to lead the way.

When you're a seeker on a journey life will give you the exact experiences you need to be able to see yourself clearly for your truth in the moment. It takes awareness and courage. It takes the discerning eye of truth to see yourself for your patterns and to hold them in the light of non-judgmental view. My lessons on this journey were coming at a speed so fast it was hard to stop long enough to reflect and change along the way. I had set out a clear intention with the Universe that 'My One' and I would be able to build our lives together in full partnership – this included working together. This experience would be the experiment to see if we could come together in this way.

It was a rocky start. My indomitable spirit began its dance of bull-dozing its way to powerful production and unceasing activity. Anamchara has a very different way, the way of reflection and winding to a conclusion by nurturing and taking time. In truth, our ways are very different. Had we had a different, less significant attachment to each other, I think we both would have ended up frustrated and completely unproductive. We learned a lot from each other, about the yin and yang of how we fit together, our strengths and weaknesses coming together in beautiful partnership. When I tried to bull-doze too quickly and move on, he would slow me down. When he meandered too long in something intangible, I would speed him up or re-direct us to move forward. It was an interesting dance of getting to know each other in an entirely different way. There were moments where it was clear that we were taking a huge risk by investing so much time and energy into this project, as the organization was somewhat out of our control. I was ready to say 'enough already' countless times as he taught me an important lesson about giving way to a process and letting it unfold in its own due time. He taught me about nurturing and tenacity when moments get difficult or when the road gets unclear. He was teaching me valuable lessons I hadn't learned along the way. Often we would stop the brutal painstaking work we were trying to accomplish simply to replenish our spirits in just a kiss. It was incredible to feel a resurgence of strength and resolve simply from exchanging our energy in a physical way. We began the negotiation of sharing work space and balancing it with relationship space.

I gave my all to this project and when it was finished I felt pleased and proud of my efforts. I had seen myself step into a passionate vision and see it as far as I could. For one of the very first times in my life, I did everything I could from start to finish. I brought my brilliance and shone in its light.

When we started this project, we knew that he would be leaving on a trip out of town right before it was due to be sent in for project approval. He was leaving, and I was stuck in the middle of making sure it got completely done. If I hadn't known in advance this was going to happen I think I would have gotten really angry at his departure. I had given too much again, in a space that wasn't mine. It wasn't my project, it wasn't my vision or dream and honestly, I wouldn't have gotten one single thing out of its successful completion except the knowing that I contributed to him being one step closer to building his dream. That would have been enough, I think. It was such an ingrained pattern in me that I stepped into it without even thinking. I had done it again, gotten totally consumed in the energy of another, I had used up all the energy I might have been directing to my own life.

We had spent three entire weeks consumed in one

way or another with each other. We talked multiple times every day, he would call out of the blue and we'd talk about dreams and hopes and even little glimpses of what might have been our future. His energy was as passionate about me, as mine was about him. Towards the end of our time together I finally shared with him my life intention statements I had written a couple months before. I felt it was time for him to see exactly where I wanted to head. While it never mentions his name, the writing was on the wall. It was the life I wanted to create with him. It was the life I wanted to create for myself, for us and for our children. It was a combination of all the things I believed were important to him in his life partner and all the things that were important to me. It might have been nice or even considerate for me to have included him in all my wishful intending for the future I wanted us to have together. But instead I chose passive aggressive nonchalance in determining what our future together would look like, without him. If he registered the duality of my actions, he never commented on it.

In our final few conversations before he left on his trip, he started talking about my dreams and about my goal for my life work. He talked about how he had spent a good deal of time thinking about where we might put it on his property or that perhaps we could buy an adjacent property next to his. He talked animatedly about how we might be able to partner together to build both his dreams and mine, side by side. I remember thinking at the time, "Hey wait a minute, here I am slaving away on your dream and instead of helping me build your dream, you're lost in fantasy about mine, the dream I'm not really ready to build yet and we're on a deadline here..." It was clear to me in these conversations, the diversion tactics even as he spoke them. Anamchara was afraid of stepping in to his own brilliance. I believed in him more than he believed in himself. I was doing most of the physical work on this project and he was stepping out of reality and smack into the fantasy of my dreams. I was flattered, if not stunned and it felt to me that he had finally turned the corner and could see the possibility of our future together.

It is so much easier for some of us to believe in another more than we believe in ourselves. It's certainly something I've lived my life doing. I can see the shining brilliance in another long before even a minor shimmer of my own reaches my consciousness. It takes grit and determination to silence the Wicked Ego Witch and stand in the center of your own Divine Truth to see yourself for exactly who and what you are.

When he left on his trip, I fell into an abyss. I was mentally exhausted from all the energetic effort I had expended on his project. I was emotionally exhausted from all the relationship energy we'd built together over the last several weeks. In one way, I was glad he was gone. In another way I was completely lost without him. I knew that it was time to contact my Seer again.

3/23/09 - We started the session as always, with a prayer for the highest and greatest good to come from what would be revealed to me and I asked the same question I always ask... "What do you see?" She saw me very clearly rising up, as a flower opening – "A red gold goddess of pure power – the emerging experience of infinite power being created with the ripple effects re-framing my life." She was also very clear about relationship pictures our souls were showing at this moment in time. "Stuck in fear pictures" – old energy patterns." For the Anamchara, "It's going to suck me in." For me, "I'm going to lose him." The patterns keep coming up so it's time to look and see what's the healing here? She was very clear, adamant in fact that I would not lose him, that we have free-will. The quality of our connection and commitment was too strong. This time was about trusting spirit, and having love and compassion for self. We are beautiful mirrors for each other – that our challenge of this time was not to give into fear pictures. It was clear that husks were peeling off, layers of healing were happening and that we were dropping away of old things that no longer served us. Our journey was to "Remember who we are – trust in our own Divine plan and trust that spirit has it all dialed in. We are to go with the flow staying present, conscious and using our tools." I asked my Seer about our future which I had done before. In the first session where I had asked about my relationship with the Anamchara she was not able to see our future, the picture was veiled. This time she saw something much different. "The veil is now translucent. She saw a road, wandering hills with a gorgeous sunset filled sky of red/purple and gold. She saw the path – the hills rolling, not mountainous. And she saw our twin souls, turning to flame as they come into union – expanding the Universe." She sighed and said "It is a very beautiful picture."

When I first started opening up to alternate realities, or explanations for what was happening around me, it was an interesting dance. It would have been ridiculously easy for me to dismiss whatever my Seer told me as fantasy or illusion. But, when I listened with my inner Truth, my own Divine Knowing, the pictures became clear. Its truth was so absolute that the Wicked Ego Witch couldn't even bother to start her litany of inadequacy, fear and shame. I was learning to trust more and more my experiences with the Seer. The opening picture she showed me was the complete truth, I had stepped into my own goddess of pure power with the project Anamchara and I had been working on. I had remembered my Divine Truth to be brilliant and had brought the very best I had to give from a space of powerful creating energy, and the results had been phenomenal.

The relationship space issues the Seer showed me were also completely in line with what was happening between us. During our weekend, we had taken a break from the monotony of the work we were doing and got into one of our most profound and intense conversations. Somewhere in the middle of that conversation, I climbed up on his lap as he whispered in my ear, "I don't want to get lost again, I don't want to lose myself in you. You wouldn't want me that way." I knew exactly what he meant because, at that moment in time, I was already there. I was drowning in my fear pictures and drowning in my thoughts that I would lose him.

The two weeks he was gone were filled with dramatic ups and downs. At the top of the roller coaster I was high on the love and connection we had built together. At the bottom, I was fraught with the Wicked Ego Witch and her rants of inadequacy and fear. I started questioning the energy and effort I had been putting into the relationship. I began my dance of fear that I was going to repeat my own tragic history of sabotaging the relationship I had waited my whole life to have. I know my own patterns. They are crystal clear. I can hold on forever to a man who won't commit, right up until he does. When he falls in love with me that's when something shifts inside me that I can't control and my feelings shut off. I was terrified I was going to break my Anamchara's heart. I felt him coming to the table of love and starting to fall in love with me. The energy in him had shifted. I could feel the difference in his touch. I could see it in his eyes, the words were not necessary and it scared me to death. I was terrified and my Wicked Ego Witch capitalized on my moments of weakness. I begged and pleaded with myself to slow down, stay centered and to stay present with the moments that were happening in my life without him. Sometimes it worked; mostly it did not. I hadn't come as far as I thought though, and that was difficult to comprehend.

Shortly before he came home I had another vision. This one came to me in a dream. This dream was so real, so honest and true that I couldn't discount it as subconscious longing. Anamchara appeared in a dream and only spoke three words. His face was so clear, so peaceful and so full of love that when I woke I was certain I would find him laying wrapped up next to me. He said, "You are My One," and he smiled and disappeared. I woke up immediately and was filled with a profound and intense peace and knowing. I drifted off smiling and returned to sleep.

Two Steps Forward, Three Steps back.....

Through this journey I have been introduced to my most egocentric self. I hadn't really owned, nor appreciated the level of egocentricity that I possess. While I try to be selfless and giving, Mother Theresa I am not. Not even close. I expected, hoped I guess is a better word, that Anamchara would return to me professing his undying love and we'd sail off happily into the sunset. Right until my Wicked Ego Witch played her dirty tricks and my feelings shut themselves off against him. I expected that immediately upon his return he'd call, like within the first five minutes of having the telephone available to him. We had gotten so close before he left and had talked so many times a day on the phone, that I really hoped that he had missed me with the intensity that I had missed him.

The phone did not ring. It didn't ring the second day he was back. I could control myself no longer from the righteous indignation I felt at not being the first thing he thought of when he returned. I picked up the phone in a burst of little girl temper tantrum and called him first. Pleasantries opened the conversation, and he talked of gifts he thought of buying me, and some that he had actually brought home. He said all the right things I guess, but the energy had shifted again. I could feel it. Perhaps it was my energy, the energy of the cavernous hole that was beginning to believe that no matter what he did, or how often he showed up, it would never be enough. Nothing and no one ever had been enough. Nothing or no one ever could be enough. I felt light years behind where I thought I had gotten. For as many steps forward as I had taken on my spiritual journey to myself, I found myself at least that many backwards. I was straight back in the place I had been for all of the relationships that had come before. I was insecure, fraught with anxiety and waiting hyperactively, for the other shoe to fall.

I woke up with a start, drenched in sweat and shaking the night after I talked to Anamchara on the phone. It was her, the Dark Horse who had called to me in my dreams. I could feel her, as if I'd become one with her. We were standing together on a rocky butte staring dead in the face of a mountain lion. Unable to move, frozen in terror I felt her adrenalin and fear coursing through my own veins. In my dream, the mountain lion gave no warning before it took flight in ferocious fury and landed, with its razor sharp claws digging deeply into her back. Her frenzied cries of terror burst through my lungs and across the coal black desert sky in warning to her herd to stay away. I woke just as her huge black body folded underneath her and she went down, struggling for breath in the sand beneath her.

Anamchara was distant in his return. Very likely it is as he says, that he returned to enormous business chaos after being gone so long. My little girl and the Wicked Ego Witch didn't buy it, because it was after all, in my egocentric relationship perspective of the moment, only about me. Boy did the little girl and the Wicked Ego Witch have a field day with this. I was tormented and tortured by my own mind. I was spun right back to the point in time that I swore I would never love again. I was planning for the end. I knew it was coming. The voice of Spirit inside me was silenced.

In the truth of retrospection something had changed. He didn't come back to me with the intensity he left with. While I don't know what happened to him on his trip, nor what he was thinking or feeling at the time it's fair to say I believe he fell into the same trap that I did. Fear. Anamchara and I have very similar relationship stories. Our patterns are very close to the same. It is part of our energetic resonance with each other, part of our soul agreement with each other to heal. I didn't know that at the time, at least not in the way I know it now, but even then, I could feel the fear and hesitancy radiate through his being.

I hate the little half truths we tell ourselves and others when we're too afraid to stand in our own Truth. My relationship with Anamchara had been built on honor, integrity and connection to each other. My little girl started screaming loudly to have her needs met, from that selfish insecure place she finds herself in from years of not having her own voice and standing in her own center of power. When my little girl gets her panties in a bunch, I am still often caught off guard and unknowing until I am smack in the middle of cleaning up her messes.

About a week after Anamchara came home, on a beautiful sunny early spring day, I decided I needed to see him again, right this minute, today. The half-truth comes in the tale I spun to explain why I was suddenly in a town, on a workday, so far from home. The building I worked in was unexpectedly having some roofing done. The smell from the tar began making everyone in the building faint and sick. A fellow manager and I decided we would close down the building and send everyone home. Serendipity, I could exit gracefully and start my trek down the highway. The little girl was overjoyed at her triumph. I called his work, and tried to get a message to him to see if he might be free for lunch. I left my town before getting his answer telling myself the sideways lie that it was a gorgeous day for a drive, and either way, I wouldn't care if I got to see him or not. I kept driving and the phone didn't ring. I got about 30 minutes from his town and called again. For some odd reason, he actually answered the phone. I told him I had to be half way between his town and mine for a meeting and I had decided to just keep going. I shuddered at my half-truth as the words came out of my mouth. Damn little girl, now my conscious was taking a beating. Lie or not, he was free and very shortly I pulled up to find him waiting. We hadn't seen each other in a few weeks.

The moment I saw him again, it was the same, the pure connection happened and then we were off. We had a nice time together, enjoying a meal and light-hearted conversation in the spring sunlight. The laughter came easily again with the spark of togetherness that I craved. It was all there. But something inside of me wouldn't be satisfied. Our time together was short lived, a simple day trip and shortly after our time started, it ended again. I beat myself up for the journey the entire way home. I felt like I was forcing things, pushing my agenda as I always did. It didn't matter that he appeared to be genuinely happy to see me. It didn't matter that we had a great time. No, nothing was good enough for me in the days of the spin to the end.

Boundary Dance...

I didn't know until my relationship with Anamchara that I had zero boundaries for getting my needs met. I was too afraid to ask. I didn't have appropriate boundaries for myself and I had no clue at all how to ask respectfully that my needs in a relationship with another be honored. I think for me it always came back to being afraid to ask, because if I asked for what I needed, and the answer was no what was I left with? I was left alone, because at that juncture I'd have no choice but to leave. I knew myself well enough to know I could never draw a line in the sand that I, myself would refuse to cross.

Is that where all the desperation and neediness came from? Not standing in my own Truth and being too afraid to ask for what I needed? When had I decided that I didn't have the right to ask, and that my demands were too much to be respected? These questions began to tumble through my mind. I had no clue what my boundaries even were. What did I really want, in my heart of hearts and what negotiation could I live with to stay in partnership with this man I'd grown so quickly and so all-encompassing in love with?

I've come to understand that boundaries should be flexible. They should be a part of the negotiation in relationship. It doesn't matter if we're talking about work, children or romantic relationship, boundaries can and should be flexible. Dixie, my horse, had started to teach me that lesson. When had I forgotten?

It was time I became clear about what my relationship boundaries really were. I spent some time thinking about what my relationship really looked like, and at what times I felt really needy and out of control. Had I ever asked Anamchara for what I needed to feel safe in our growing partnership together? I really hadn't. We had a few "deal breaker" conversations but those were so mind-numbingly obvious, and completely impossible between us, they seemed silly to say out loud. Things like, if you ever hurt my children, if you ever physically hurt me, that type of thing. Those elements didn't exist in our relationship, period. We had never had a conversation about getting our individual needs met as two separate people living two separate lives. When I reflected on what I needed, it really seemed very simple. I needed him to make an effort to connect with me on a regular basis, in a perfect world, every day. In reality, every couple days was something I could live with. I needed him to make the time to take initiative to plan things for us to do like, taking the initiative to plan a weekend or whatever. I felt like I was doing all the planning. I needed to feel him bringing his energy to the relationship. Usually, he did these things. It's just when his life got chaotic, he would stop. There should have been a part of me that understood that, but when his distance came, my little girl would start her temper tantrums. My Wicked Ego Witch was iron-clad in her ranting that I just simply didn't deserve his respectful consideration.

If you don't ask for what you need, people just won't know. Every once in awhile I would flare up and say something out loud about the timing between phone calls and he would respond, which left me laughing for as evolved as I believed him to be, "Sometimes I am just a dumb guy and I need help knowing what you need." He'd even opened the door to me speaking my truth, and I felt if I did I'd be perceived as yet another woman with too many needs to fill. As I starting thinking through and getting clear about my lack of boundaries I felt it was time to have an open conversation with him, if for no other reason than to force myself to say what I needed out loud.

He called really late one night after I'd left him a message that I wanted to talk. For the first time ever, I had to force myself to wake up enough to engage in our conversation. I knew what I needed to say, and I really just didn't want to. I could see Radical Faith in the distant reflection in the alarm clock light as she raised her sword giving me the gentle nudge to put down my emotional wall and say what I needed to say. Our conversation began and lasted the better part of three hours. I went on autopilot as the stories of my relationship past and feelings of inadequacy tumbled out of my mouth like a woman gone mad. I went all the way to the pit of my past relationship space and even said to him, "I feel like I'm trying to talk myself out of a relationship with you." Of all the things I said that night, that is the only thing he really remembers. I talked about being afraid of hurting him, I talked about my patterns of getting a man to love me and running away. I opened my dark side wide and silently begged him not to turn away.

Our conversation came back around to him and I asked him where he was at with what was happening between us. His first sentence shocked me. "I am in awe of you. You have everything – body, mind, heart, spirit. You are the whole package I am looking for." He went on to talk about the place inside of him that still, "just did not know" where our relationship was headed. He admitted that he felt uncomfortable with the level of intimacy we had been sharing to this point, which I assume meant both physically and emotionally. He rambled endlessly that he was still missing a "knowing" that indescribable thing that whispers "Yes, she is the One." As a very spiritual man, he felt that he should know by now if we were meant to be life partners. He didn't know that we shouldn't be, but he didn't know for certain that we should. He talked in long and winding tales about his ex-wife, and his sense of knowing her so completely so early on, and how, after time and children, he had been so wrong. I could hear the wistful lilt in his voice as he talked about her.

Standing outside in the pale half moon light, listening to him talk in circles I felt overcome by an ethereal presence. I could feel her again, the Dark Horse Satori. I could feel her anxiety, her false expectations and her pride. I could feel her hesitancy to step into something new and unknown. Just as she dashed away from my consciousness, he abruptly ended our phone call.

The Ebb and Flow of the River…

My birthday was fast approaching and I only had one real wish: to spend it with my Anamchara. But beneath the superficial 'I want to spend my birthday with you' what did I really hunger for? I wanted him to profess his undying love and in doing so, to quench all my fears in the nectar of happily ever after. I wanted his eyes to penetrate so deeply that I could see his very soul of truth, longing and desire to be with me forever. I wanted my little girl to play with his little boy every day of our lives. I wanted the damned Wicked Ego Witch to be proven wrong. I wanted to know that I was worthy of love, that I was really good enough and that finally I had found the one who was never going to leave me.

Anamchara did engage a little more, and called a few days in a row. I was feeling like maybe we were getting back to the relationship intimacy we had found before he left for his trip a few weeks earlier. Coincidentally, if there is even such a thing as coincidence, I had been invited to attend a meeting that was to be held in his town. It was a meeting about horse welfare, which is my passion and I felt the Universe must be smiling its divinity on our luck. I decided to go down for the meeting the night before and stay in the his house.

When we met this time, his energy was different again. He was forlorn and withdrawn. I couldn't find the sparkle and promise that was usually held in his gaze. Our conversation was half-halted and seemed to ramble along making no coherent sense. Often we just sat quietly, neither saying a word. In a real relationship, those moments of silence I've been told, are the spaces that hold knowing and connection. Still caught in my egocentric insecurity, I withdrew from him completely and into my own private hell of self-doubt. During those quiet spaces of our meal, I found myself thinking about what our lives might be like on a daily basis caught with his frequent bouts of self-reflection and withdrawal. He has his own story, his own set of emotions and his own daily life challenges that have absolutely nothing to do with me. The fact that he is chaotic and frequently upside down and in crisis, is just part of his story and the reality he has created for his life. I started asking myself some internal questions. "Did I really want to be in a relationship with a man whose life was always so upside down?" I started looking with a bit more discerning eye at the truth of the man that he was showing me. For so long I'd been enraptured with his essence. I often overlooked with mild amusement his reality. I tried really hard in the early days not to place him on an untenable pedestal. I thought I had been successful.

When our realities of my insecurities, and probably his own, matched up with our physical distance from each other and his chaotic tendencies – what did we have left that would support a real life as two human beings, together?

Relationships ebb and flow. They sail high and they sink low. I became excruciatingly clear that I had no concept of riding the tide of relationship reality. I have never been able to nurture a relationship to long term success through the daily grind we call life. That's part of the beauty of learning to exist in the present, to be completely in sync with exactly what is happening in whatever moment in time I found myself, not pining away for the past (which wasn't all the great to begin with) and what it was before, or in the future wishing on what it might be.

We mostly just bumped along and for the very first time in our relationship, had nothing to say to each other at all. I think we both half-heartedly tried to connect to each other, but for the most part it was elusive. My birthday had passed earlier in the week and somewhere along our drive he reached across my lap, opened the glove compartment and pulled out a box. "Here, open it," was all that he said. The box contained a necklace with a huge stone pendant. Carved into the pendant was a long haired woman and a horse combined and flowing together. It's held together with a chain of hand carved Peruvian beads. It is simple and ornate all at the same time, as the horse and the woman blend together so that it's impossible to tell where one ends and the other begins. Holding the necklace between my hands, I could feel the energy and spirit that radiated from the stone. He said he had called out to the Universe to find the perfect gift for my birthday. He had, it was perfect. When I looked down at the necklace again, I could see us, Satori and me. The emotion that swept through me and broke through to my consciousness was the fear we evoked in this man.

When we made it back to his house I could feel

the weight of my own emotional distance. It was crushing. Our entire relationship to this point had been built on our spiritual connection to each other. To have that missing was excruciatingly obvious and incredibly heartbreaking. He left his house to walk to the barn to feed, but for some reason, I chose not to go with him needing a few minutes to try to settle myself for the evening that lay ahead. I became so overcome with insecurity that I literally felt the little girl take rise. I could almost hear her say, "There must be something lying around that would explain his behavior." I've learned nothing if I haven't learned this. When I seek, I always find. It doesn't matter what I found, my mind would make it support whatever I thought would be there in the first place.

Like a long lost and long overdue beacon of light I felt my rational adult stand up and take control, or perhaps it was just simply fear. I wasn't going to look for anything. In fact, I took great strides to make sure I didn't. I turned off every light and pulled the rocking chair in front of the door and sat, quietly rocking in the dark staring out at the trees. It was in that moment that I realized I could set boundaries for myself and I could keep them when I did set them. It was a moment of triumph, however trivial, that I honored myself and Anamchara by respecting his privacy and doing the right thing.

When he walked back up to the porch he sat down beside me in the doorway. It was a beautiful night with the clouds parting way to reveal the stars scattered across the black desert sky. Putting his head in my lap he began to talk, and open up, loosening the strangle-hold he had held on himself for our entire day. We talked for hours in deep spiritually connected conversation. We never talked once about our relationship but we talked intensely about ourselves. He had been hurt a few days before in a fall off of one of his horses. He wasn't hurt badly but years of unhealthy habits, age and pushing himself too far had taken its toll. We started talking about how difficult it is to grow older and have our bodies begin to shift and change revealing our neglect along the way. With self-hatred comes physical brutality. It seems a little harsh written on the words of a page but blended over a lifetime, innocent destructive habits become patterns clouded with the dust of neglect until the body can take no more and it breaks down. Our conversation flowed around and around until we found ourselves on common ground together again. I could understand his physical weariness, because I could feel my own. It was a barring of the truth of our humanity to each other – our realness at being spiritual beings contained in a body with its own limitations and of being trapped in the most dangerous neighborhood of all, the six inches located directly between our own ears.

We talked of how our spiritual desires seemed to be limited by who and what we are physically or by what we were thinking about at the time. It was a profound discussion and through it we found that spiritual connection again. It was as strong and as intimate as it had ever been. It was simply part of the ebb and flow of relationship. I learned a very healthy lesson that night. I learned about my egocentric viewpoint of another in a relationship with me. His distance had to do with his own set of lessons and his own personal journey. Part of being in an honest, spiritual relationship with another is learning to honor their journey as well as our own. Relationships are an opportunity, a mirror, if held in just the right light, to see our Truth, our Self if only we are brave enough not to cast the shadow back at our partner. When we are in relationship with another, regardless of its definition, its purpose is to help us learn, heal and grow ourselves. Anamchara held the mirror up so I could gaze into it with love, compassion and grace. I was learning to be brave enough to consider the insights to myself, a gift.

As the evening drew to a close, weary and talked out, we climbed into his bed. We were both quiet, reserved and thoughtful. Because our evening together didn't have the same threads of romance I was used to I climbed into his bed fully clothed and he did the same. After moments of snuggling close, our clothes were lost to a man and woman ready to find each other in a different way. For some reason, very contrary to my nature I took control and found myself returning the gift of physical passion and attention he had given so freely to me in the beach house. I allowed myself to explore his every nuance as a man, as my lover as my soul mate. For me, this was a first. I can be egocentric in many ways.

I became fully present and completely in tuned to his needs as a man. I put aside my own needs and centered my concentration completely on him. It was incredibly beautiful for me. I had finally found my sexual voice. I finally found my own internal passion that asks that we give, more than we receive. And in giving, I found my Truth. He sighed softly and whispered his gratitude to me in saying, "I haven't been loved like that in decades." For a passionate man, these words filled my insecure Wicked Ego Witch completely into silence and contentment.

The Facets of Family...

Anamchara is an incredible father. One of the most amazing lessons he was teaching me was how to be really present for my children, to really see them, for who and what they are as spiritual beings traveling their own individual journeys. He was teaching me how to take the time to slow down, play and savor every minute I was blessed enough to have with them, something I had taken for granted for far too long. For as much as I had been an attentive, caring provider to my children, my role with them was very parental. I think when you're a single mother you swing one of two ways. You either, blur the boundaries between parent and child and become more like friends or you become both mother and father and become the sole provider and authoritarian. I became the latter. It's a ridiculously hard thing to balance at least it is for me. To those who are able to successfully negotiate both roles, and become parent and friend, my hat is off to you. It's a journey I am still in the middle of.

He would talk about his experiences with his children and his values for raising them. I would listen to the way he talked to them with total loving attention and kindness. A part of my heart would melt listening to them share together intimate father, children moments. I carried a desperate hope that one day my children would be able to call such a man their very own. It was something I had never been able to provide them. There was always laughter and presence in his voice whenever his children were in the room, an attention and focus that couldn't be denied, not even separated by a telephone wire. While I had spoken to his children on the phone, we hadn't made the decision yet to bring our families together. It was time.

Partially in honor of my birthday, he decided to bring his children up to play in my city. We decided to take all of our kids and go out to enjoy something new together. I was torn in half. Part of me was ridiculously excited to meet the people who were the very most important thing in his life. The other part of me was terrified. The usual questions, would they like me? Would our children get along? What would the energy be like with all of us all together? I knew how our families blended together, was a make or break point in the relationship. If it felt wrong, or his children had strong negative opinions I knew the end to our relationship would shortly follow.

True to the ebb and flow of our relationship, we let the evening unfold before us. I led the way winding around the crowded streets until I came to the park blocks located in the very heart of the city. In the very center of the park block is a playground that has huge metal elephant sculpture that stretched up over a story high. It begged to be climbed on, I could see our children hanging from its huge statuesque trunk and draped over its massive belly. Rolling with the atmosphere and praying the kids would be so enamored with the elephant that they would forget all about me, I parked the car.

I was humble and tidy in my first moment of meeting his kids. Trying hard to keep up my pretense of parental perfection I greeted each of his children with the kind of lavish attention they are used to. I was immediately struck by the inner light and essences which seemed to radiate from every pore in their being. It is the kind of light that shines in a child who has been allowed to be exactly who and what they are and encouraged with unconditional positive regard. They simply sparkled from the inside out. They radiated warmth, openness and adventure. They have their father's mischievous sparkly, dancing eyes.

The first moments passed quickly and we set off to find adventure. We ambled quietly, his children close by his side, and mine close to me. The curse of my womanhood is the incurable overactive bladder which rears its ugly head at the most inopportune times. I asked Anamchara if I could run inside a bar that seemed to be the only place open on the entire street. It had huge windows that opened to the street side. Peering inside, we noticed there were a few families with kids eating at tables scattered around the distance of the open bar. So we decided to go inside. Yes, that's correct. We took our children, by accident into a bar. It was a fancy affair that catered to the neo-yuppie jet set. It was shimmery and loaded with televisions and computers. The kids were fascinated by the ambiance while I was fascinated with them. As we sat around the table, the kids started interacting with each other playing games on my cell phone. With their faces huddled together, we sat across the table watching our children develop their own ties to each other. For me, it was a magical dinner that shone brightly with possibility. It felt very, very real, and very, very right. I could see for one moment in time what our families blended together would look like. In truth, I adored his children. In a way, the oldest reminds me much of myself. She reminds me of the little girl I once was, so full of magic, mystical adventure and fearless courage to try anything. I would have loved the opportunity to spend time with just her, exploring the world through her eyes to be reminded further of all the things my little girl has given up in the process of growing up. My children were fabulous, entertaining and full of charm. It didn't go unnoticed to me that when I stepped aside as the authoritarian parent and allowed them to just be who and what they are that I could see them in such a different light and enjoy them in such a different way. It was an incredible experience for me to set aside my "role" and just simply be with my children, with my Anamchara and his.

We left the bar and headed back to the huge elephant waiting patiently in the park blocks. We laughed, we played. We climbed, played chase and keep away and I allowed myself the rare opportunity to play as the child I once had been. We watched our children playing together. I watched his children take risks and climb mountains. I watched my children watch in envy. When had I taken away their courage to try new things? All the times I said to them, "Be careful, it's dangerous, you could get hurt," flashed through my mind, it was another lesson on my journey. I realized how my actions and intentions, thoughts and fears were creating experiences and life perceptions in my children. Now that I knew better, I was going to have to do better.

Our evening came to an end as the sun began to set, a drunk plopped down unconscious in the park grass and a prostitute sat down on the bench beside the Anamchara and me. In one momentous burst of protective energy, we rounded up our children and left the park blocks downtown. It should have been a warning, how things can change in an instant. The minute the sun set into the sky, and darkness surrounded us, the entire vibe of the park blocks morphed into something dark and dangerous. We'd had a really good time together, as two people sharing our children and allowing them the opportunity to make new friends and have a night away from the usual routines we were accustomed to. We just weren't ready for the night to end, so we decided to see a movie. Popcorn in hand, we all settled in to watch an adventure show at the very top row of the IMAX theatre.

Usually Anamchara and I couldn't keep our hands off each other. Of course, I understand the necessity for caution and timeliness' when you are introducing children to each other and to the potential of a new relationship. I knew intellectually the need for us to appear to our children as just friends. When the lights went down I tried to snuggle in discretely, touching at least at our feet and felt, for the first time, Anamchara keep his physical distance. I was heartbroken. It registered, and I tried to dismiss it but nagging deep inside was the feeling that something had changed.

Our evening ended with hugs to all, and promises to see each other again soon. My kids were immediately asleep in the car on the drive home so I had time to think. I had just been given a beautiful, tangible gift of seeing what our family could have really looked like. My fears about his children had been washed away. They were simply delightful, and our children blended together in the beautiful way that children can do, with Effortless Grace. What happened between Anamchara and I couldn't really be explained. In some moments, we would get lost in each other's eyes. In other moments there was a cloud of grey. I couldn't let go of the little voice that said, "Something is about to change."

The Warrior and his Bride Return...

Anamchara and I talked a couple times by email after our evening with the children together. I still couldn't shake my nagging feeling that something was just around the corner. Out of nowhere my mood became sullen and my temper, violent. I went to bed one night with a fury coursing through my veins. I had no reason, none at all, just a fury lighting its way through my consciousness that I hadn't felt in years. A few hours later I woke up and saw an email from Anamchara asking me to review a business email he had drafted. He wanted my professional opinion about its content. As I read the email my fury raged. Other than the email caption which said "Tell me what you think sweetness." There was no other personalization other than, "Would you mind?" Hell yes I minded. I don't know what I minded about, but the fury wouldn't be contained. I went back to sleep without answering his email and figured by morning my crazy dark mood would be gone. I was wrong. I woke with the same vengeance I had fallen asleep with. I started to type a response to his email and then decided to wait a bit longer. Email can be a tricky venue when used in a moment of anger, passion or delusion. A few hours later I typed him an email full of what I thought at the time, was contained anger. It said,

I think --I am not sweet at all today.
I think -- that it would have been nice for you to send a yes/no email regarding my phone message to pick up a saddle for me before asking me to proof read for you.
I think -- I have taught you that it's ok for you to ignore my needs and only come to the table at your convenience, when I have whined so much it's obvious I need something or when you need something in return.
I think -- I'm done with that.
And yes I realize this comes out of "nowhere" but it only takes one last straw to break the camel's back. Today, mine feels broken. - my fault, not having good boundaries and drawing the line in the "how I need to be treated" sand long ago.

I think -- I am tired of taking all the responsibility and doing all the apologizing.
I think-I am pissed off and done watching my woman bend over backwards and have no self-respect
I think - I am pretty clear my little girls tantrums are because she's failed to have clear and consistent boundaries
I think- My little girl is screaming to hit delete.
I think - My little boy says "Wow.. it's about fucking time."

My boundaries were bound to come out one way or another. My email made them very clear. I was tired. I was tired of giving too much, I was angry – at me, for doing the exact same thing in relationship space I'd always done. I was tired of feeling like I was doing all the work and he wasn't. I was finally just angry. The anger however was aimed at the wrong person. When I sent the email I think I was just trying to release the powder keg that I had bottled up inside of me. A few minutes later he sent me back a response. He said we needed to talk, that he was leaving for a meeting and would call me later.

The call came early and he said, "Bravo. Bravo for finally standing up for yourself it was a long time overdue." Rushed and hurried he had opened my email hoping I had done as I always did, step in and give my advice about a business matter. He said his day had been horrible and that in between meetings he jumped online hoping I had given him the information he needed. And then he said, "I was crushed. Your email just sent me reeling. I read it over and over again trying to figure out where the venom was coming from. I realized it wasn't as bad as I thought." I finally took a deep breath in hope that my darkness could be shifted back to something positive but there was something hanging in his voice, a controlled ice I could hear through the phone line. The conversation continued and finally he said, "I know what needs to happen now. I know." Baiting him I said, "Ok, what do you know?" He said, "I know that I don't think you are the person I am meant to be with as my life-partner." Oh my God. Catastrophic.

The Wicked Ego Witch roared in hilarious laughter and I told you so as the tears of never being good enough, grief and loss streamed down my face. The conversation twisted and turned several times, so many times that I began to feel the possibility of hope that our relationship wasn't actually going to end, but maybe that was just wishful thinking. He kept saying, "You were trying to talk yourself out of our relationship a couple weeks ago, say something that can help me talk myself back in."

I could feel him trying to hold on, I could feel the weight of confusion in his voice. I asked him, "What is it that you know now, what's different?" His only answer was, "I know from my highest level of spiritual truth that my woman is saying no to us taking this relationship any farther." As a deeply spiritual man, he could only answer in the terms of which he viewed the world. His woman, of the four sides of direction was for him the sage, the spiritual guide. I said, "Could she be wrong?" And he replied, "Not at this moment, I don't know down the road. I know you are everything I could have possibly ever wanted, you have everything. I just don't have that one thing, that knowing that it's you." Part of me wanted to start screaming and yelling. What? What the hell? Your woman? What does that mean? The other part of me knew that he held his spiritual beliefs so tightly that no matter what I said, he was going to stand on his truth as he understood it. I simply just couldn't argue, and frankly had come too far to try. I tried really hard to get him to say something concrete, something tangible I could live with. How do you explain the unexplainable? I'd been there before, been in relationships that I had wanted to work out, but that thing, that intangible thing that makes it last forever just wasn't there.

For some bizarre reason he started talking about percentages of being sure of his decision. He went on to say, he was 80% sure. Of course, I jumped on the 20% remaining and needed to know what that meant. "It means that 80% of me is listening to my highest spiritual truth of knowing right now, the other 20% is the possibility the knowing could change or develop over time." I asked him, "What if you figure out you're wrong?" He answered immediately and with a strength and conviction that couldn't be explained away, "I would find you I would call every telephone number, show up at your door and wait until I could talk to you. Nothing could keep me from saying I'll be there in 2.5 hours."

Staring off in the distance of my backyard I could see her again, the Dark Horse, Satori. Why did she keep showing up in my mind? Every time she'd appear I'd be thinking the same thing, about Anamchara and about fear. The pieces finally fell together. Satori, his Dark Horse, is his horse of fear. Between the surreal conversation I was having with him and Satori showing herself to me again it all became so clear. I knew with every fiber of my being that he was being driven by his own fear, his fear of what was possible – to have everything he ever wanted. And I knew enough to know there was nothing I could say, no way to manipulate the conversation to change the outcome. He had opened the door for me to try to change his mind, to say something, anything, to change the outcome. Out of respect for him, for who I had become and for the journey I knew I was taking, I couldn't.

The waterfall I was in on my River of Life became Niagara Falls in a moment. Flipping out of my boat I started flailing around, smashing against the endless boulders of doubt, shame and rejection. In a free fall tumble I couldn't stop the flood of grief. I couldn't stop the tears. I was transported to another time and place, and my reaction to our conversation was way out of proportion to what was happening. So what? So Anamchara was scared. I could talk him out of it? Couldn't I?

Through my tears I got an overwhelming feeling for

the very first time in my life. I had to go completely away. Our relationship had to be 100% over. No communication, no friendship, just over. I said to him, "I can't do this. I have to walk completely away from you forever." The words flew out of my mouth, as if possessed by something completely outside of me. Then he became hysterical, he started sobbing loud and uncontrollably, I could hear his heart-shattering anguish through the phone wire that held us together. And then they showed themselves to me again, the Warrior and his Heart Song Bride. I could see their faces', feel their grief and the miles that separated them.

"Talk to me through your tears," I begged him. I needed to understand why he was so emotionally distraught - he was the one ending the possibility of our relationship. What was driving his irrational reaction? I begged him, "Please, please tell me what's behind your tears?" He sobbed louder and louder. Then I knew. In hushed tones I whispered over and over again, "Oh my God, Oh my God, the Warrior." I could finally see the truth in the story behind the Warrior and his Bride.

The last time the Warrior and his Bride had shown themselves to me was through Anamchara's tears, on our first weekend together. I had written about it in my letter to him so long ago. It was all flashing in front of my eyes. I was grief stricken in a way I had never experienced, Anamchara, sobbing – the two of us only connected by a telephone line and it all became so clear. In a surreal slide show through my mind I could see pictures flashing in rapid succession. Pictures of the Warrior bloody and broken, watching his Bride from the distance of a surrounding hillside, standing defeated and in shame. I could feel his emotions coursing through my veins. And then I knew, the Warrior lifetime was ours, Anamchara and I. I had been the Warrior in that lifetime, and he had been the Bride. My sight was about us, in another time and place, a place where we had loved each other completely and had lost each other entirely due to grief and limitation. In that moment it was so clear, so real that I wasn't even standing in my human reality.

Anamchara said it was his woman, his highest Truth who was saying we were not meant to pursue a life partnership together. It was her. She was too afraid. I could feel through his confused agony the weight of her grief. The Warrior left her, not trusting in the love they shared for each other and she would not allow that mistake to be repeated again in this lifetime. The resonance of that lifetime was playing out again, in this one. I begged him to listen to me, to hear the story again. I said, "It's your woman, she is still too afraid to love again." I had known it all along, the fear that we both carry. The connection we had to each other was too strong, too real, too encompassing for the short journey we had taken together so far in this lifetime. But he couldn't hear me. He was too lost in his own truth, his own knowing and his own fear and pain.

The end of the conversation was brutal. There was nothing more I could do. I was shattered. He was just gone. Neither one of us could hang up the telephone. I knew when the line went dead that our relationship and any possibility of a future together, even as friends, would be gone as well. I begged him to hang up, because I couldn't do it, and eventually the silence turned to the buzz of a line gone dead.

Sobbing quietly I closed my eyes, in my grief I must have dozed off. I found myself standing on a rocky butte looking down on the rugged ledge below me when I saw the Dark Horse again. The nightmare of the mountain lion returned. Her dark body shuddered in the moonlight as the mountain lion opened his jaws, in a single swift and decisive movement sunk his teeth into her flesh and she was gone.

The Choice…

After the line that held us together went silent, I had a choice to make. I had learned throughout this journey that I had spent far too many years of my life in a dead-walking stupor. I had intentionally stopped feeling any emotions because I was certain they would drown me alive if I felt them. At this cross roads I had a choice. Do I sit in the middle of my overwhelming grief and let it come or was I willing to stuff it all inside and go back to being who I was before the journey.

There was no decision to make. I had traveled too far to be shoved back into a way of living that no longer fit for me. I could finally see that my lifeboat in the River was beached on the rocky shore after the waterfall of madness that had come with our end, had taken me over. Having been so far I knew my only hope was to gently coax my lifeboat back into the River and continue on. It was there I made the conscious decision to sit in the middle of my grief.

There were moments when I was on my knees, shaking and trembling with a visceral pain that was all consuming. Still I sat. I let the grief wash over me in billowing, overwhelming waves. I would try to stand up and get knocked back down again. Sometimes I would just stare. I would sit in the backyard, in my chair and just stare at the trees begging them to whisper some quiet wisdom that might alleviate just a fraction of the intense crushing pain I felt. Somewhere, somehow, this had to make sense. And then I'd stop trying to make it make sense. I could only own for me, what was mine to own. I couldn't change Anamchara's mind. I couldn't make him find the courage to face his own fears. I couldn't make him see what I could see so clearly. I had to respect his journey. I had to respect my own. Something inside of me was entirely different. The Wicked Ego Witch was stunned into silence.

For the first time in my entire life, I knew that the end of this relationship had absolutely nothing to do with me. I did everything right. I found the courage to move through my fears. I took the risk to fall in love when the outcome was so unclear. I learned how to engage my inner child, laugh, play and appreciate the life and gifts I had been given. I started to become a better mother. And I knew, beyond a shadow of a doubt, that I would have the courage to love again. The journey that came with my Anamchara and my desire to move through the experience with grace and courage, gave me my life back and I wasn't going to give up the gifts I had been so graciously given without a fight. In my spasms of grief it was hard to feel Radical Faith but in those quiet moments when I was simply too tired to think anymore, I could sense her golden presence drifting high among the trees I was begging for answers. She was there as an ethereal resolve, that kept my heart beating in my chest reminding me of all the blessings I had been shown in the journey.

That's all great stuff. Intellectually, I was very clear that I had learned far more beautiful things than I had lost in my relationship with Anamchara, but emotionally and spiritually I was flat-lined. I had to learn to ride the ebb and flow of emotion. I had to learn that whatever emotion came to the surface would eventually subside. I had begun the dance of letting go.

He called the next night, in a gracious attempt to see if I was ok. I answered the phone because I needed to see if he was still so sure of his decision because in the end, there had been such new light, at least for me as the Warrior and his Bride appeared again. He was gracious and kind, and we talked for the better part of an hour. I asked him again why he was so overcome with emotion at the end of our conversation. He said, "I just never thought I would lose you. You are too important to me." I tried to explain why I couldn't be casual friends with him. I just couldn't. We tried to talk rationally about my sight of the Warrior and his Bride but because he couldn't see what I could see, I think it only made a minimal intellectual impact. I don't think he discounts the vision. In fact, I believe he knows it to be true, but it wasn't making a difference in this time and place between us. He said repeatedly that he would wait for a time for me to be comfortable, and that his door would always be open. He talked about not knowing what the road ahead between us might bring.

That is really the truth of all relationships. As humans I believe we have this excruciating desire to label our stuff and this absolutely includes people. Marriages end every day in divorce. Happily ever after turns to screaming matches and child support. There is never a forever, not in any relationship. They shift and change over time. We are never guaranteed anything from one moment to the next. This journey for all of us sharing this lifetime is transitory. I had a delicate balance to find. On one hand, Anamchara was still saying, "Stay open." On the other, he had closed the door to the future I believed we were destined to have shared. With my tendencies to hang on to relationships for far too long, this was a dangerous open ended dilemma. I think part of the reason I was so adamant that I couldn't remain friends with him was because I knew I would constantly be looking for that inroad, that manipulation to more. And in doing so, I would set myself up for continued heartbreak. I had it happen a 1000 times, in a thousand less significant relationships. I knew myself too well.

The relationship I shared with Anamchara was always, from the very beginning otherworldly. There was always something more to the story. My intuition was too strong to be discounted. I was grief stricken and heartbroken and I needed more insight. I needed to understand. I needed to be able to put what happened in a neat little box and put it back on the shelf of memories with the rest of the love affairs I had left behind. I needed to talk to my Seer again. Your soul will always give you the Truth you are ready to hear.

Karma...

I was honestly scared to death to call my Seer on the day we were scheduled to talk. I gathered all my sacred objects and candles that I used sometimes to pray and before I made the phone call, said a prayer for myself that whatever would be revealed to me, be only of the highest and greatest good.

4/29/09 - As always I opened the conversation with asking my Seer the question, "What did she see?" She saw compassion, compassion for self. I was in a pivotal point for quantum shift change which was very positive, much like the one I had gone through after the ranch sold. In my space she saw "An acorn – shiny, solid and small. I was shifting viscerally through amazing growth of becoming spirit." She said the space was very uncomfortable, that my body personality was letting go of illusions of an old paradigm that I was trying to fit a rainbow into a tiny space.

I asked her to go into my relationship space. She immediately said, "The two of you have very interesting karma of many past lives together." She hadn't ever said that before in the two previous times we'd talked about my relationship with the Anamchara. She said in most of our lifetimes, Anamchara had shown up had the male body personality and me as the female. She flashed to a lifetime she called Lumiria. This lifetime was in the age of the planet Atlantis. She described the space in great detail. Lumiria was a lost planet, highly evolved with a society built around a power grid of crystals. People were hungry for power and the planet became so out of balance that eventually it was lost. She said in this lifetime, Anamchara was a scientist type who was working on trying to access the power of the planet. At some point, he got caught up by higher-ups who were after personal gain. He became very torn, he knew right from wrong but was caught in a situation where he had no choice but to leave. If he didn't leave, he would have been killed.

I was a member of a "goddess temple" – a spiritual structure that worshipped the Divine, she likened it to the spiritual societies of the ancient Greek. In this place I knew something was bothering him. I loved him deeply in this lifetime and had a choice to go with him or stay in my own life as a spiritual being. I chose to stay in my own life and let him go away without me. I knew it was the right decision for me but I always questioned my decision and got stuck in the energy of the relationship that had to end. I didn't trust myself or honor my loss. I was never able to heal and move forward. Anamchara in this past lifetime moved into a "wounding space" where he was unable to bring up the guilt, shame and self-judgment. He left without me.

I have to admit, when I was in the middle of this time with the Seer, as she was telling this story I had a hard time believing it. It seemed very far-fetched, but the threads of the journey I had just taken with Anamchara seemed to resonate with some of the issues she mentioned. The Seer continued.

You shared another lifetime in the year 1736. The Warrior and his Heart Song Bride. There it was. This was the lifetime I was shown so vividly throughout my journey with my Anamchara and in one word, the Seer confirmed what I knew in the last moments with Anamchara were true. In this lifetime, we had traded roles. I showed up as the man, the Warrior—and Anamchara as the Bride. She confirmed for me the visions that I saw throughout the relationship Anamchara and I had shared. The Warrior and his Bride lived and loved completely. In a time of tribal war, the Warrior had been attacked. In this attack, he was left horribly disfigured. In his own limitation he made the decision to abandon his Bride because in his heart he believed she couldn't love him any longer. He spent his lifetime watching over her from a distance. The Bride stayed trapped in her grief, in a cycle of endless waiting for him to return. Her broken heart was the legacy she left behind.

The Seer said that we had carried and played out the same themes in more than three lifetimes. In this current lifetime our souls had made a full agreement to do pieces of our work individually, in our relationship together. She said, "The work isn't complete, you had the opportunity to get it and you both made progress with it, there are lots of layers to the journey of your spirits."

She continued,, "In this past lifetime, The Warrior and the Bride, you got very clear about your judgments of self-worth. You got very clear about limiting yourself. You came out of that lifetime with the very clear agreement that you would not limit yourself in the dance of karma again."

I asked her about Anamchara and where he was at spiritually at that moment, she entered his space briefly, and this is what she said. *"I can see him in a room with padded walls. He doesn't see the door. He is consumed with grief and rage. He is so disconnected that he doesn't trust himself to find his way out."*

We talked about the 'full soul agreement' that the Anamchara and I had agreed upon in this lifetime. Our agreement with each other was to grow ourselves. We created situations where we had the ability to confront and heal those places inside ourselves that needed attention. The intention to do this, for us both, was so strong. My role in this lifetime was in my knowing that I would not limit myself again. I would not lose myself, rather, find myself in my own truth and spiritual knowing.

The karma for Anamchara in our relationship was around confronting his limitation pictures. What the Seer said next, leveled me. *"Your reaction to the end of this relationship was visceral, I CANT DO THIS ANYMORE. Your grief contains all the lifetimes before. You are grieving now for lifetimes of loss with this soul. These are powerful pieces that you are taking to a larger karmic paradigm. As a spirit you need to ask yourself, does the dance with this soul continue to serve you? Not from a place of judgment, but rather, have I learned my piece?"*

The Seer and I looked at the agreement and possibilities we had in this lifetime. Anamchara and I could have chosen to get it right. The agreement was made. We could have lived in this lifetime together as partners and soul mates. That was possible. The Seer said that for me, "It was an intention, a beautiful picture that was the very real possibility of relationship nirvana." For Anamchara, the picture was an illusion. He never believed it was possible. She said, "He has the picture but it's like a fairy tale, it is not tangible for him. He doesn't believe it is possible."

She said, "He could have been the one, but your primary agreement in this lifetime is to yourself and your growth. You can't do it for him. In the end, you are clear that you have said no to a dynamic that no longer serves you. In this lifetime you will not sacrifice. It is time to grieve all the lifetimes before. Grieve what could have been and grieve all the times before where you didn't make the choice for Self."

In this lifetime part of my soul's healing was to release the energetic burden I've carried around stored grief, staying energetically in a space that was too small for my continued spiritual growth and not being able to let go. In past lifetimes I'd held on to lost love, like in the Lumiria lifetime. In the Warrior lifetime, I had held on to my own grief and shame of being too broken and feeling limited by the tragedy that had befallen me and the Bride that I had left behind. In this lifetime, I had a choice. I had the choice to let go and move on. The one thing I'd struggled my entire life with doing. I could never let go.

We talked more about the Anamchara in the context of our current relationship, The Seer said, "He had the chance to face his fear and make a different choice. He is not ready. He is comfortable in his familiar patterns. To move forward requires a willingness to jump. You made the choice to jump he's not even on the dock."

I asked her about the possibility of our future together

and what she said should have come as no surprise. She said, "You both have the power of free will, any choices are possible. In this lifetime she saw about an 18% possibility that things for Anamchara could shift but at this time, she didn't see me with him, his space was too small for what I had become." She saw me "Coming to a peaceful heart." I asked her about staying connected with him as friends, as he wanted and her response? "It doesn't serve you other than salt in the wound. You won't grieve."

I really needed to know what she saw this relationship had provided to me, what was the healing supposed to be? For me this relationship with Anamchara was about seeing how "I limit myself in relationships and take on what isn't mine."

She said, "He received healing and lessons as well. It is up to his spiritual truth to understand and integrate what he needed to receive. He is back in his old story, turning his attention to do the same things. He has his own reaction to what happens. It's a limiting story, but his dance in this lifetime. She said "You have expanded as a result of this soul agreement. The possibility is there for him as well."

As my conversation with my Seer ended she commented on what a tremendous growth experience this had been from me, that I was learning to live in a more open and expansive spiritual place.

Honestly, at that moment, I didn't care. I was crushed and devastated. Everything made so much sense, and was almost heartbreaking in the cruelty of being faced with the reality that even from lifetimes before Anamchara and I were destined, at least in this moment in time to walk away from each other again. I could feel the weight of those lifetimes. I could feel the grief wash over me in re-doubled effort. The only small consolation was at least I now knew why. Knowing why made it harder, not easier. Now that I knew the truth, of this lifetime and all the ones before I was faced with the only choice I could make, to really, truly walk away. Something continued to haunt me though, it just didn't feel right. I would cling to the notion that if Anamchara only knew, something might change for him. Ah, the desperate attempts my ego made to try to make this make sense.

When you are learning to walk in two different realities you feel almost crazy. I mean that literally. Every piece of rational media, human knowing in the 21st century would flood my thoughts. "This is insane," I would think. How could I possibly be really living karma? I was stuck, grieving and completely unsure of what to do next. I was spinning in that scary place of knowing what I had to do, and being completely unsure I knew how to take the first step. I had to talk to Anamchara again.

The Dance of Goodbye...

Sitting across the table from me, resplendent in her leather clad glory, the Wicked Ego Witch polished her razor sharp nails a deep blood red. This magic spell was purely writing on the wall and required no particular effort from her at all. In my desperation I clung to the notion that I could be Anamchara's savior – if he only would just listen to the truth I now possessed. How could he not hear me? How could he not know the words I wanted to speak to him out loud about our karma were true? How could it not make a difference in our outcome? We were meant to be together in this lifetime, weren't we?

As I heard his voice on the answering machine a wave of real truth swept over me. Radical Faith was poised fiercely with her bejeweled sword held high. Her message was clear. It was simply time to believe -- in me. It was time to walk the road of my own redemption and soul journey not bound with another that clearly wasn't ready to take the journey with me. As I placed the phone in the cradle, the slender, soft golden arms of Effortless Grace surrounded me once again. Cradled against her I knew I was not alone and the peace in that knowing allowed me to breathe freely once again. I knew what I had to do.

The Seer had been clear with me that sharing the knowledge I had been given with Anamchara should only be offered as a gift to him, not a re-engagement in an old dynamic of trying to hold on to a space that was too small but I felt like I had to say the words. I felt like I had to face him again to say good-bye. The relationship we had was too intense to be ended on the telephone. It almost seemed like the easy way out.

I received an email from him the next day saying he would call me later that evening. I spun off into a frenzy of not knowing what I would say when the phone finally rang. I called my best friend to try to gain some perspective. She told me to find a book, preferably the Bible if I had one, open it up and read the first page I came to. She said that contained on the pages I would find some wisdom to help guide me until the time came to hear his voice again.

A few months earlier, my life coach had told me about a book, one she thought I should read called, 'Broken Open' by Elizabeth Lesser. She tried to give me the nutshell version of the book at the time but I dismissed her. Broken Open? Hell, I was finally starting to heal and live again. I didn't know what the book would have to offer me. As my relationship with Anamchara was ending, I started to connect more intensely with another good friend of mine who was in the middle of making the decision to divorce her husband. The day before I called Anamchara she said, "You need to read the book 'Broken Open.'" There it was again. When the Universe hands you a gift and the message keeps repeating itself, it's time to pay attention. As fate would have it, I had bought this book earlier in the day.

I climbed into bed and reached for 'Broken Open' and began to read as my friend suggested. One of the first stories in the book was about the author traveling to see a psychic. The story she tells in the book had me so incredulous all I could say was "Oh my God," over and over again. In this vignette she talks about her marriage ending and her affair with a "Shaman Lover." She traveled to see a psychic. During the reading the psychic told her about the soul agreements and karma she was living. It was the same conversation, with practically the same language I had just had with my Seer. I was stunned speechless. It was as if Divinity itself was screaming loudly, "What you just heard and read is true… pay attention… do the right thing… let go of the karma…" I must have read that section fifty times waiting for the phone to ring. It was going to, I just had no idea what I would say when it did.

I needed closure. I needed to see Anamchara again, look him in the eyes and speak my truth. I needed to see his truth. I needed to look in his eyes and know for sure that what he was saying was true. I needed to see that the connection was broken and that it was time to let go. I needed to be in his space, knowing what I knew from all our lifetimes past, and see the window to those worlds close so I could move on. What I was doing was giving away my power again, to him. I was leaving it up to him for me to decide to move on. I needed to see something in him that would give me the strength to walk away. What I wanted was to see something entirely different. What I wanted was to see was the truth of our lifetimes of love in his eyes. I wanted him to see me. I wanted him to "know" something different. I wanted him to say he was wrong. I wanted to hold on forever. Letting go of lifetimes of being a certain way isn't easy and you take as many detours as direct routes to get to the healing necessary to move on. I hoped I was ready to let go, but deep in my heart of hearts, I wasn't.

The phone rang late, as usual, and wracked with nerves I answered the phone. Lighthearted and almost frivolously, his voice greeted me. It was as if nothing had changed between us at all, the ebb and flow of the conversation was effortless as he led me on with word play.

It's an interesting thing to be so very desperate to hear something specific that no matter what is said, you get the inference you were looking for. He said he wished I had been there with him, that he was in a mood to go out and play and stay up all night talking and if he had been a drinking man, to drink Meade. I had no idea what Meade was, and as he explained it, he made yet another reference to marriage. In a winding story Anamchara told me that Meade was made for the wedding night back centuries ago. Over and over again, at our race to the finish, he would make comments about things that had to do with being married. It was the weirdest thing. But of course, when you are seeking something specific, you will always find reference to what you're seeking. Our conversation wound around until I finally found the courage to say two things. First, I told him that I wanted to see him again, I didn't say for what purpose and he didn't ask. The second thing I told him was that I had a gift for him and that it would always be available whenever he felt like he needed to ask for it. I was referring to the Knowing, the gift of having our karmic circle revealed to him.

Shortly after my conversation with the Seer, I sat down and wrote out the entirety of our relationship in karmic cycle and set it aside to give to him if he ever asked to see it. The Seer had told me, "If you choose to share your knowledge, do so as a gift, not as a reengagement in an old dynamic." I felt he had the right to have it, since it applied to him as well as me but he would have to choose the right time to receive it. If he ever did ask for it, he'd receive it, no questions asked. I trusted that if there was a place on his journey where the information would bring him healing, light and growth, he would just know.

He told me that the day after our relationship ended he found a note that I had left for him. The note that said, "I will find you again in the moonlight, in another time and place…" I left him this note our very first weekend together. He hadn't found it, until the very end. We ended the conversation with me saying, "I've been clear that I want to see you again to talk. I'll leave it up to you to decide when." And we hung up the phone one more time.

The next week passed by at a snail's pace with my river of grief washing over me in torrents of hurricane strength. I had no idea how I was going to live without him. I had no idea how I was ever going to love again. I had no idea how any other man could possibly get even get remotely close to the standards of passion, emotion and spiritual connection we had shared in our time together. I was standing in quick sand and losing ground fast.

To Know the Truth…

A few days after my last phone call with Anamchara I was standing outside in the late afternoon of a gorgeous early spring day. Part of returning to my life was simply finding my own magic in the purely mundane. Staring off towards the grandmother evergreens that I had been so much a part of my letting go journey I was filled with a sense of clarity that I had never known before. The Truth, unabashed and unadorned I now knew. Throughout my entire relationship with this man I had felt certain that he would come to love me as I did him and that true to my own relationship patterns, I would walk away. This thought terrified me, as if its course was already written in history and I was powerless to stop it. In a flash of light I knew the truth, but what I knew, came too late. I was completely in love with this man and I knew with absolute conviction that I would have done anything and everything to have built our life together to last. I would have never left him.

When the thought, "I would have never left him," tumbled through my mind I was struck with such a Divine presence and Truth that for a good long while my lifeboat was righted again. I was sailing smoothly down my River of Life in a Universal Truth I had never known before. I am capable of loving. I am capable of building a life together with another human being. I am capable of committing and living in a life partnership with my One. Everything I had ever believed about myself and relationships disappeared in a current and was pulled out and swept away over the waterfall in the River. It was no longer true, and I knew it with every fiber of my being. I knew it so clearly that it didn't matter that my relationship with Anamchara had ended. It wasn't about him. It was, about him, but my highest Truth knew that no matter what had happened between us, I would go on to love again and I would be able to build the partnership I finally knew I deserved. My Wicked Ego Witch had been called out and seen for her truth and her lies. Her cackles of laughter disappeared in the current as they too, were swept into the river and drifted quietly over the waterfall of life.

The Warrior left his Bride in our past lifetime. I had spent my entire life creating the same theme over and over again, in every relationship I had ever had. The karma and cycle was broken in my Knowing of my Truth. And I will never let it re-create its hateful and destructive patterns again.

I sat down and typed an email to him, of my Truth. I no longer needed to see him to say goodbye. I needed to speak my Truth, stand my ground and let go to the Universe to unfold its next life lesson.

Anamchara, I have to try -- one last time. In the beginning you wrote me these words "I would regret allowing you to fade away without putting forth every effort," -- it was those words that changed the course of history for me. I write these last words hoping, that once again -- karma will step in and move us together. This journey with you has been spectacular -- and the lessons profound and life changing. I am not the same wom-

an who responded reluctantly to your gentle persuasion. I have learned so much about me, what was holding me back -- I've learned the "truths" I carried about who and what I am were wrong. I learned that I can open my heart -- I can embrace my passion... ahh so many good things. Here is my truth. I fell completely 100% in love with you, every little tiny nuance of the man that you are. I would have never said it possible. You challenged me on my very foundational beliefs about what love looks like, what it feels like and what I want my future with my one to look like. You opened the door to family, to building dreams, to speaking from the soul. To walk away from this without telling you the whole truth would be a grave injustice to what we have together. I kicked and screamed, fought with my own shadow, pushed through my own fears to come to my foundational truth. I didn't even know what that was until certain points on the journey... The whole time we were together, I would get really scared about hurting you. I was terrified that one day, you would love me back and I would do exactly what I've done every other time -- run away. It took losing you to know how very wrong I was. I would have loved you completely until my very last breath. I would have given us -- our family -- everything I had in complete open-hearted love. I would have pursued my passions and helped you build yours. I would have laughed, cried and held on. I didn't know this until very, very recently. I am so very - very sad that it might well be too late. Together we found "the forever one" - the one who would have never left, the one strong enough to move through all the bull-shit of life -- we found the soul connection, the "knowing". You found it too. And it's in fear that we lose it. It is so clear to me when things changed -- things changed immediately after three weeks of becoming so close, so intertwined that we were virtually one. It changed when I "spoke my truth" -- when I told you what I was so afraid of -- loving you. When I told you that I was "trying to talk myself out of a relationship" - *I know what you heard because I know you. -- You heard the fear, the questioning and your own fear came up to overwhelm and crush us. My truth is very clear. We had it. Together we found what we'd both been looking for -- and it showed up so perfectly, so complete that it was utterly terrifying. I had a job to do -- a journey to take. And I have, I did. It was the journey to love. I don't have any idea what you'll do with this -- it just had to be said. It's actually not what I wanted to say to you before -- before, it was goodbye. But over the last few days, and ending with a dream last night it became clear that to walk away from you completely without trying one more time would have caused me to wonder the rest of my days if I could have done or said something -- in my own power and truth which could have changed things.*

I am very clear that I can't be casual friends with you. I just can't. For me, unfortunately and heartbreakingly it is really all or nothing. If indeed our time has come to an end, I need to be completely free to walk into my future. I can't make you change your mind or break through your own fears. I can only wish you all the love in my heart that your journey move forward -- the same wish I have for myself. Just as you would have done if I hadn't answered your first email, I will do. I won't contact you again. The future and the next contact will have to come from you. The door is open. I love you with a huge heart ready to say yes. If you chose this to be the end, please know there are three doors I leave open to you forever:

1. If you choose to accept the Gift I will have if for you without any strings attached from now until my last breath. When you need it, you'll know and I'll give it freely.

2. If you ever need anything only I can give you. Please be compassionate and wise about asking but I will be here.

3. And finally, if you ever "know" - that you'll be at my door in 2.5 hours. PLEASE do not be too afraid to make that call, or show up. I don't know what the conver-

sation would be or the end result -- but please, just as I've done here - bring your truth. Don't be afraid. I will love you until the very last breath and hold you in a place of compassion, truth and healing. For me, I walk into my future with an open heart and clear road -- I hope that it will be with you..

Until then...

Anamchara Returns...

Out of nowhere, Anamchara showed up a couple days later to send me an instant message via the internet. He asked what I was doing for the weekend. Shock radiated down my entire nervous system. My response was the only thing I could muster in the moment. "Why?" I typed. He answered, "I'm heading your way." Again, my only response could be "Why?" He continued, "First, to see you. Second, there is a gathering up your way and its Mothers Day weekend." I answered, "I have no plans at this point, what are you thinking?" His response surprised me, "Maybe we could grab a bite Friday night." I answered, "You apparently haven't read my email. Maybe you should and then you can decide about Friday." And as quickly as he'd thrown it out there, he was gone. I was reeling. Hope surged and as quickly, was replaced by skepticism and negativity. What could he possibly want? I would have to wait to find out.

Friday rolled around, and I received a brief instant message that he was busy in meetings but trying to get out of town. He said that he had read my email and left it at that. All I could do was wait to see what our reunion would bring. The phone didn't ring until well after 9pm and he said he'd be here in 2.5 hours. Hope again tried to reach the surface of my rock solid fortitude and just as quickly was replaced by the simple truth that I didn't think anything had changed. I had to be prepared for anything. I went through every single possibility I could think of. The Wicked Ego Witch threw in every sideways, backwards, horrendous thing she could think of to get me to change my mind and stay home. As the clock neared 11:15pm I left the house to meet him. I tried to stay calm. I tried to stay neutral and unattached to any possible outcome. I wanted to hope, I wanted to believe. At this point my lifeboat had a terminal tear in its foundation and I was taking on water faster than I could bail it out.

As I pulled into our meeting spot I glanced up and realized it was a full moon. We were meeting again in the moonlight, in another time and place. This wasn't at all what I had in mind. Hope surged again. And this time I allowed it, for the briefest flicker of possibility that it might have contained.

When my car pulled up he was waiting. I climbed out, and so did he. He grabbed me into a huge hug. I know he could feel me shaking. I couldn't find any words. Numbness had overtaken my brain. I still just wanted to run. It felt bizarre to feel awkward around him. In my entire life, I had never been around any other human being who felt so right, someone with whom it was so easy to be just who and what I was. We decided to find a quiet place to talk. By now it was after midnight and choices were limited. The 24-hour diner didn't seem appropriate so we decided on a local resort hotel known for good food and home grown distillery that was just up the road. We left in two separate cars. The entire short drive I remember the psychotic conversation of thoughts flooding my brain. "What do I say, what's he going to say?" And then, in between the incessant mental chatter the silence of the space of possibility showed brightly just under the full moon. I just had to keep walking forward and be open to whatever came. Was I strong enough to do this? At this point I had no choice but to find out.

We got out of our cars and he reached for my hand. He nestled it in the crook of his arm and we walked into the full moon, cold late spring night. We got a couple of drinks and settled into a picnic table. Facing me, I could see into the center of his soul through his eyes. I guess I needed to see for myself his determination to end our relationship. I needed to be convinced that he really was sure that something that felt so right wasn't the direction he wanted to travel with me any further.

The minute we sat down he said, "I love you. I adore you, but I am still sure that I am not meant to have a life-partnership with you." I felt my heart crush again, and the tears well to spill down my cheeks. I could feel the sting of the pain brutally cold against my skin. In the last email I sent to him, and verified with him that he had read, I had given him three clear doors back into my life. They were very specific. Otherwise, I asked him to let me move on. Meeting me in the moonlight, just to walk away again, wasn't one of the reasons. I finally was able to form words, "You read my email, where I was very specific. Why are you here?" It was almost an accusation. It felt like one. I felt baited and switched. He answered, "Because you said you wanted to see me and because I needed to see in your eyes your determination to really walk away from what we have forever." Our eyes were locked intently into each other's gaze in our space of eternal knowing with each other.

As much as I wanted to see something different I said, "When I look into your eyes, all I see is fear. I don't see the truth of us ending as much as I wish that I did. It'd be so much easier if you'd just say to me, "Your ass is too big, there's someone else or your breath stinks. Anything, any reason would be good enough, better than I just can't explain it." He roared with laughter. "Okay, pick one – how about the third choice whatever that was. It's just that random. There is no reason, I just can't explain it. It's a knowing that just isn't there." "Its fear," I said. "When I look into your eyes I see everything, desire, connection, emotion and then fear. I can't fight with fear. I can't make you move through something you aren't willing to see."

The mood between us became heart-wrenching and somber. To know something so clearly – like the sky is blue or the grass is green but to not be able to explain why it's so—felt tragic. There was so much love radiating between us under the full moon cold night air, but all I could feel was the irony. He said, "I hate this. I don't want to date anymore, I hate dating. Maybe I was meant to be alone to carry out my life vision. I want to be in a life-partnership but maybe that's not what was meant to happen. You aren't the first intuitive woman to come into my life to tell me about fear. There must be something there that I can't see. Maybe I just can't right now."

He got up to go to the bathroom and in a beautiful burst of protectiveness asked me to move closer to the restaurant where there was an open pit fire surrounded by late night guests. It was beautiful respite from the cold steel frigid numbness I was feeling surround my heart. I had come so far in my journey to open my heart that I became consciously aware of the tightening that I could feel like a vice grip starting to take hold. Out of feint amusement, I picked up my things and moved over closer to the fire hoping to end the cold chill I couldn't seem to escape. He said intently, but quietly "God, you are so fucking gorgeous…" and walked into the bar. I could feel Radical Faith and Effortless Grace standing somewhere in the shadows beneath the trees that surrounded the fire pit but I couldn't find them. My ears had gone deaf and my heart was beginning to shut down. I was on my own, because I chose to be.

I walked inside to find him warm in the restaurant ordering another hot chocolate. He looked at me with eyes so penetrating that it was totally obvious which side of his brain was taking over. Was I going to let it? Chemistry is a bizarre thing. I honestly don't think we get to choose. It's either there, or its not and the chemistry I have with this man rivals no other I'd ever experienced. I knew what was coming but I truly believed we both were responsible enough to control our more base attraction to each other. He leaned in closer and closer and our eyes locked in another realm all together. We left the safety and warmth of the restaurant to go back to our picnic bench. He sat next to me, huddled under my coat for warmth. It took less than five minutes for the impossible to happen, the kiss I had waited my whole life to experience happened again. It was fire. Absolute fire. I could honestly kiss this man every minute of my life, for the entire rest of it and be absolutely and completely satisfied. That is no exaggeration and it is completely mutual. We got swept away in our own time and space. It didn't matter that it was closing time, it didn't matter people were flooding out all around us. The only thing that mattered was the kiss, the complete intoxication of our lips coming together. We did sexual gymnastics fully clothed all over that bench to the point a reserved security guard interrupted, "Hummhh.. excuse me. We have to close down, could go to your room now?" I was horrified, amused and hysterical but horrified. Anamchara thanked the guard for his polite interruption as I tried to hide my face in my hair. Some things never change, we'd been there before.

Together we faced the crossroads. What now? Which was really a stupid question considering that what now, was very clear. There wasn't one part of me that wasn't completely certain about what needed to happen next. It was right, it was natural, it felt good and I wasn't going to regret one single moment the next morning. I don't know how or why I knew that, I just did. Of course, the conversation had to happen and he was just as clear as me, "No regrets, none."

As we walked into the hotel Anamchara called me "Mi alma" – my soul – it's what he'd always called me. The very same words he chose to call me in his email that started this journey so long ago. As we were checking in, the hotel concierge asked him if I was his wife. Wife?

Anamchara looked at me, smiled and said, "Yes." It felt so right and I felt so honored that for a moment in time I was with the man I was supposed to be with in this lifetime. He honored me with the gift of saying out loud, our relationship has value, she is my one, if only for tonight.

The rest of the brief night was spent in passion. It was beautiful, it was erotic. It was everything it had ever been and a glimmer of something more. We held on to each other with a passion uncontained. We laughed and played and made love to each other for hours. Unfortunately, I knew that I had to get home very early to my kids and we hadn't given each other any opportunity to sleep. As the minutes grew closer for me to leave it became clear that we hadn't gotten any farther on closure. Nothing had changed. He was on his side of the wall and I was on the mine. I knew I needed to walk away completely. I was too involved emotionally to be able to shift to casual friendship. The last half hour I tried to get him to talk, I needed to walk away free with the space closed up so that I could move on. We clung to each other, we cried. It was heartbreaking. The last words I said to him were, "I will always love you Anamchara." And all he said to me in return was, "Anamchara." My last memory of this heartbreaking morning is of him standing in the window, naked, looking out at the sunrise as I walked out the door.

I know what I said in the email I sent him, and I meant it. I meant what I said about it being too painful to stay connected in a different way, a way of friendship without expectations. I always mean what I say. That's the thing about being human, which I am, very. Circumstances can change my mind. Everything that happened was surreal. It was if nothing had ever changed. Of course, I've had ex-sex before. That quiet, comfortable place of knowing your relationship has ended but something necessitates a physical union to complete the goodbye. In part, maybe that's what this had been. It didn't feel like it, and believe me I was looking at every possible angle

I could think of. Anamchara and I fell into the place we can always fall into, the absolute spiritual, emotional and physical connection of two people who have loved and lost, lifetimes before.

I knew what I had to do, the Seer had been very clear with me, that to stay connected to Anamchara would not allow me to grieve and move on. She had also said we had free will. Something about what the Seer told me didn't feel complete, like there was more to the story or perhaps an alternate ending. It's hard to dance in two worlds when you barely understand the real one you're trying to live in. Has anyone ever written anything about how to release karma? If they have, I haven't read it. I could have used it.

As I drove home, I was shattered. The grief was so real and so strong it was as if no healing or progress had been made on it at all. Something about walking completely away from Anamchara felt wrong. Perhaps that was the point of the life lesson. If it felt comfortable, maybe I was continuing an old pattern. All I know is that I felt certain that I was going to die, that I would never recover from having him lost to me forever. I didn't want to take a shower and wash his energy from my body. I didn't want to lose that last bit of his scent lingering in my hair. I never wanted the bruises from our ardent love making to disappear. I wanted to stay locked in that energetic moment with him forever. Ah, perhaps the Seer was right after all.

I am so human, that is a beautiful fact. I made the only choice I knew how to make in that moment. My brain shifted and all the sudden I knew I didn't have to live without him. I just had to really, truly let go of the expectations. I could stay connected to him. I could break the karma of the Warrior and his Heart song Bride by not walking away forever as the Warrior had done in our other lifetime. It was in staying away, and not moving on that the karmic obligation had continued. I questioned myself a 1000 times. Could I stay engaged in a neutral relationship with him, building on our strengths and true connection we had but still move on? God, I hoped the answer was yes.

When I left the hotel room I had grabbed one of our room keys. I guess I wanted to keep it as a reminder of the night. I can be very sentimental that way. The minute I made the decision that I could stay engaged and let go at the same time I knew what I had to do. I flew into the shower, washing off what had been, grabbed "The Gift" I had written for him and sped off, back to the hotel room to tell him what might be.

I went flying back in the hotel room and shook him frantically to wake him up. "I was so wrong. I don't have to walk away from you." Sleepily he grinned from ear to ear. "Tell me what happened, what changed?" he asked. I tried to explain to him that I had left feeling shattered, that my decision to walk away felt wrong and that all the sudden I knew that to walk away from him again in this lifetime would be like keeping the karmic circle spinning. The look on his face was pure little boy joy in Christmas morning. I could see the relief wash across him, I could feel the happiness radiate through his being. The sense of relief for us both was palpable. It seemed, one more time, Divinity had smiled on our union. He said to me, "I almost said the same thing to you last night about it not feeling right to walk away if that had been our destiny in the past. I didn't say it because it felt like I would have been trying to talk you into something to have things the way I wanted them." He was right. If it had been said by him the night before, I would have dismissed it. If it was to be this way, I had to come up with it on my own.

As I left the hotel room I handed him "The Gift." I said, "I brought you The Gift. It's for you to know when you are ready, if ever, to receive it. I don't want to use it as a bargaining chip to get you to come to me. It's here. It's yours to do with as you want." I left it sitting on top of his shoes and with one more kiss goodbye left the hotel room and walked back into my life leaving him behind.

Letting go...

I would love to say that it was easy to walk out of that hotel room knowing that the man that I loved was so close, to walk back into my own life. It wasn't easy at all. I felt a certain peace that I had made the right decision to re-negotiate for myself the terms of how we might have been able to stay connected. The first day was fairly easy, because I slept through most of it. The second day passed with only every other thought being of him and what I had no choice but to leave behind. The days that followed weren't much different than the second day.

I sent the Anamchara one last email that I called, "Letting Go." It was part of my journey of letting go to honor all of the hopes and dreams that I had along our way. It was also my way of paying gratitude for all that he had been in my life. I've learned that part of the journey is learning to honor ourselves and our need for closure in whatever way feels right at the time. Sometimes, that's a face to face goodbye. Other times, it's a letter or story burned in effigy of remembrance. Writing is just my way. When I hit send I knew I was ready to leave the old expectations behind and embrace wherever my journey might be taking me.

Anamchara, God I miss you. I miss the connection, the ability to pick up the phone.. I miss the hope, the dream, the possibilities. I miss the mischievous twinkle in your eyes when you're about to do something naughty. I miss the deep soulful conversation, I miss being so lost in your eyes that I can see the very depths of eternity. I miss the phone calls late at night. I miss our pure power and magnificence together, I miss our talks of building our dreams together. I miss the fireplace and the smell of your tobacco. I miss the wisdom of the trees on your lane and the whisper of the creek when I so desperately needed a connection to my own soul. I miss the way you reach for my hand, the way you can jump to heights in one single bound - surprising me every time you do it. I miss you "building a fire with me" "taking me to bed" and "sharing chocolate" over the phone. I miss my truth and security in "knowing". I miss sleeping naked next to you all night and waking to bring you coffee. I miss the way you mutter out loud in prayer when you don't know you're doing it. I miss holding the credit card receipt when you sign it. I miss putting your wallet back into your pants. It goes without saying that I miss your incredible ass. I miss the way your arm brushed so delicately and full of loving across my face. I miss you telling the gas station attendant that everything is amazing when you're with a beautiful woman. I miss laughing so hard that I sound like a horse.. and hearing your laughter ring through my very soul. I miss the feel of your hugs - so complete, so truthful they spoke volumes without a single word. I miss the way you say "ahhhh" and the way you sing and the way it feels to be wrapped tightly around you— traveling through our musical journey on the rug in front of the fire... all the funny little "you-isms" that you bring. God I miss the idea of you... I miss the idea of getting to dance with you, I miss the idea of getting to rock hunt with the kids, I miss the idea of being cuddled up around the fire as a family telling stories, I miss the idea of building our family and our lives together. I miss the idea of cooking dinner together. I miss the idea of eating calamari with you again or sharing chocolate. I miss the idea of having you make love to me fully—from all 4 directions, full of complete passion and absolute love. I miss the idea of biting into your neck and experiencing the wild un-abandoned passion that would have come (and the giggles that came when you tried to be in control...). I miss the idea of going to the beach for the weekend together alone —the one you shared with me so many times. I miss the idea of introducing you to Dixie, of having the kids ride my beautiful horse. I miss the idea of sharing my passions with you. I miss the idea of my children having you as a father figure in their lives—and all that you would have brought to them, I miss the idea of having you show me how to be a better, more loving parent. I miss the idea of traveling to other worlds with you—and experiencing this world through your eyes.. I miss the idea of watching your vision step into its destiny. I miss the idea of being with you at ceremony. I miss the idea of being the one person you needed and wanted to see after the seven days of the dark, I miss the idea of growing old with you, watching our children marry and have children of their own. God I am grateful... I am so grateful you sent me the email that said "without drama or delay"—or I would have missed this journey. I am so grateful that I answered you. I am so grateful I went out on that second date -- when I had no reason for doing it. I am so grateful that you kissed me in the rain—for in that moment, I could feel the power and the possibility—and as I recall said "you are not for the faint of heart"—even then I must have known the powerful lessons contained in accepting the journey. I am so grateful for all the times I got to feel the connection, for all the times we shared calamari, for all the times I was on the receiving end of your mischievous naughty. I am so grateful for all the times you called so late. I am grateful that I got to experience our power together. I am grateful I got to meet your children and that I got to see, for one moment in time what our family together might have looked and felt like. I am so grateful that my children got to spend time with you and in their own ways, learn so much about themselves and about others. I am grateful I got the experience of helping you think through and organize the possibilities of your incredible vision. I am so grateful I got to experience the magic of the trees and the peace and wisdom of the creek on your lane. I am so grateful we got to play in the ocean together and share an amazing sunset at the beach...I am so grateful for all the times we shared amazing meals togethereven the ones where you ate quail eggs... I am so grateful for all the times you reached out to hold my hand, I am so grateful for all the times your kisses took my breath away and for your beautiful arm brushing across my face—ah, so very sweet... I am so grateful that you were the person I was with when I learned that my heart is ok.. that you took away the fear, and held my space so beautifully that I could be ok even when I was so scared...I am so grateful for t he experience of feeling our bodies come together. I am so grateful that I got to be the one to explore you in ways you "hadn't experienced in decades". I am so grateful for being on the receiving end of your muttered prayers when you didn't know you were speaking them out loud. I am so grateful that you invited me into your circle and shared with me some of the prayers that had been offered there. I am grateful that I got to hear the spirit in the trees with you. I am so grateful for all the times when you came to me, in dreams - in spirit. I am so grateful that you actually saw ME.. behind the "fussing" behind the mask and the truth of the physical - that you see the truth and the beauty that is uniquely mine. I am so grateful that you taught me how to pray again. I am so grateful that through this experience I remembered how to feel passion and have an open heart. I am so grateful that you taught me how to love again. And I am grateful for how this experience with you and all the memories and hopes, is teaching me to let go. Just as all these beautiful moments passed, so too will the mourning and grief of all the unrealized hopes and dreams. The gratitude and the memories will remain forever, as will the place in my heart that will be forever belong only to you. Little by little I let go, sometimes the grief is so strong I crawl on my knees - other times a beautiful effortless grace makes me smile and know that no matter the outcome - things are as they are destined to be and the future is never clear until it becomes the present - and then the past. We will never know, until the moment that we know - and that can change in any instant. Such is the beauty and the irony of the journey... Thank you Anamchara—for all that was all that is and for all that will likely never be. I am forever changed and better for loving you.

I tried so hard to remember all the beautiful lessons I learned along the way with my Anamchara. I tried desperately to be present in each and every moment that the Universe handed me. I tried to see my children for the beautiful spirits that they are. I tried. Most of the time, I failed. I wanted to let go, and there were moments that I did but then the truth and the anger of what had been, and been lost would flair again. I railed against the karma that had us bound in the only way I knew how to do it. I tried desperately to figure out how to change it. My body personality was furious. I had found the one man, who I had been looking for my entire life and because of circumstances beyond my control, and agreements my soul had made with his in another time and another place, we were destined, at least for now, to be apart. That should have been comforting. I mean, how do you argue with an unalienable truth? Doesn't mean I didn't try. I felt myself holding on and trying to let go all at the same time. Most of the time it was sheer will-power not to pick up the phone or drive down to see him, thank God my ego had evolved past that. No, I tried with every ounce of my entire being to hold on instead of giving way to surrender. The harder I struggled against the current of what was, the harder it was to stay upright in my own lifeboat floating in the River of Life. With every day that passed, the struggle became just a little easier. It was easier until the phone would ring and on the other end of the line was Anamchara.

I think I did a fair job of trying to control my fantasies that he would change his mind. I think I did a fair job of accepting his phone calls for exactly what they were for him, simply a way for us to stay connected to each other. He had wanted nothing more. He never wanted to lose the deep and powerful soul connection we had with each other. What price was I paying by not letting go completely? Was this what the Seer had meant when she said, "To stay engaged with him in a space that has grown too small for you will just put salt in the wound and keep you from grieving."

And then I started thinking about expectations. I started looking back over all the ways I had limited myself by living in the future and having expectations about the way things should look. Had I been honest during my relationship with Anamchara? Had I really stood in the center of my own Truth and let our relationship find its own way without a preconceived notion of what that should look like? No, I did not. I had expectations. I had fantasies about how our life together would and should look. As the fantasies shattered, the expectations became broken rules and excuses and I became clingy and needy and all those things I thought I had worked so hard to let go of. I had learned a million lessons in my brief journey with this man, and as I was trying to let go of him, I forgot every single one of them. I could feel my heart start to close down again. I could hear the Wicked Ego Witch and her reminders about not being good enough. Through the process of learning to let go, I had to confront again, all the lessons I had thought I had learned already for good.

As I began to step more fully towards my Divine spiritual Truth the lessons became shorter and shorter to live through. I would start to walk off the road, and just as I was about to take a major detour, if I got quiet enough, I could hear Radical Faith and Effortless Grace whispering their gentle compassionate reminder to remember who I am. I would feel myself starting to slip backwards through land already covered by the past and just at the moment I'd be ready to take the first step, I could stop, knowing that if I just looked up I would see them again with their shimmering golden essences of Divine Truth. Radical Faith would say loudly, "You've already been here before. You have no further need to travel that particular journey." And in those moments I'd realize how much healing and growth I had done. I could finally hear her and make the choice stop at the crossroads with enough conviction to make the conscious choice to keep going forward instead of going backwards in time.

I've learned that no matter how many detours I had taken in my journey, I've always ended up in the same place, exactly where I was meant to be. If I chose to take the detour life offered me, it just took longer to get there. I had a choice to make with Anamchara. I could accept the journey for the road it had traveled and the beauty that had surrounded me along the way or I could take a detour back through my past and its confounding, winding, twists and turns of holding on, fighting – begging and pleading, irrational, insecure craziness like I had done so many times before. Perhaps it's just that I'm older now, the fight to hold on just didn't seem worth the round trip air fare to the exact same destination, the end. I'd come far enough to know that no matter what my actions, the end result was going to be exactly the same. Our relationship was just simply over. If I was ready to face myself and the expectations I held about the Anamchara, I could continue to stay engaged in a different way of being with him. That is a part of the journey that the Anamchara and I tried to negotiate. When I got really quiet, and I opened myself to my own Divine truth and the voice it spoke when I listened, I still heard the same message, "Stay open, believe…"

With every day that's passed since the last time I saw him, the stranglehold of obsessive pleas to keep him bound to me forever started to loosen. But it's only because of the grace notes that happened along the way.

Grace Notes...

There was this middle place in grief, where I was consumed – every single moment of every single day where I could think of nothing else but what I had lost. Standing smack in the middle of this place, I chose to surrender. I chose to stand in the epicenter of my own worst nightmare and allow the hurricane to knock me over. It was an act of faith and courage I didn't know I was capable of committing. I cried, I laughed, I relived every single moment of every single breath we'd ever shared together. I replayed conversations, emotions, fears and hopes and dreams. One by one I tossed them in the river of grief and allowed them to pass quietly out from under my lifeboat. Replacing what I'd thrown overboard were the grace notes that showed up as Radical Faith, Effortless Grace and girlfriends.

I am incredibly blessed to have had truly amazing soul partners, girlfriends, to walk with me every step of this journey. I must admit in looking back, that these two friends were unlikely partners on the journey in many ways.

I've had the same best girlfriend for most of my life. We met in our last year of high school and have literally grown up together. Our relationship hasn't been easy; there is no question about that. When you're trying to negotiate growing up, taking your own journey and balancing the needs of another, there is no question it's hard. My best friend and I have this crazy ability to truly see and call out our patterns in each other, and often that got brutal. We both carry years of history, opinions and stories to speak the light of historical truth with each other. The thing is that history makes us who we are, until we choose to shine the light of our own unique Divine Truth on it and make the choice to make it something different.

I am a giver. Anyone who has a close relationship with me would likely agree. If I have any kind of relationship with you, I will give you the shirt off my back and my belt, jeans and under-ware too if you really need it. I will return every phone call, usually within minutes, answer any email and be there – no matter what, if I can be. Not only in romantic relationship do I give too much, but in every relationship I give too much of myself, historically speaking anyway. Every relationship we enter into, with another human being, regardless of its definition teaches us something about ourselves. The lessons I learned with Anamchara were lessons that decades of history with people in my life could have taught me along the way. Something about being in a romantic relationship just ups the ante. I never realized how much of myself I gave away in relationships. Until this retrospective journey I had no idea I had done it over and over again.

Two years before Anamchara, I had come to a place with my best friend where I needed to draw the boundary of protection for myself. It was the first time that I have ever said, "Enough. I can't engage in this relationship anymore." She was the first.

I had to draw a boundary for myself in our 20 year friendship just as I was leaving to bring my daughter home from overseas, two years before the Anamchara crashed upon my shore. I had no choice but to walk away from her, and our relationship, to protect myself and to keep myself centered and balanced for the journey I was about to take to bring my daughter home to our family. My best friend's life had become unpredictable and I feared for her safety. In part I think I walked away because of my own expectations of what I thought her choices and behaviors should have been. I was afraid for her. I was getting ready to take the biggest risk I had ever taken to fly overseas and bring a child into my family. My own journey at the time was terrifying enough, and at the same time my best friend needed me to be her rock of sanity. I couldn't do both. For the first time, I chose my own journey.

I still carry the weight of guilt for abandoning my

best friend when she probably needed me more than at any other time in our relationship. But, in hindsight we both now know the power that staying true to my own journey would give us both. I learned how to draw a boundary for myself. I experienced for the first time what it means to stand in my own center of Truth and power and make the best decision I could make for me. I didn't, for the first time ever, divert my needs and journey to be what someone else needed me to be. She learned that she could stand on her own two feet and make the best choices for herself without any guidance. She learned how to be powerful and strong, centered and balanced through what she was experiencing. She ended up moving through many issues that had held her back for her entire lifetime – and she did it because that was the road she needed to take and she needed to do it alone.

As my relationship with Anamchara began, my best friend and I had started to scratch the surface of repairing the friendship we had shared together for so long. We had begun talking but only polite platitudes of conversation that barely scratched the surface of the lifetime we had spent together. We avoided all topics that could have gotten back to the level of intimacy we once had shared. There was a time when we knew every little nuance that can be shared between women. We could predict with 99% accuracy each other's behaviors in any given situation. There used to be a time when we could and did tell each other absolutely everything. But those times had passed with the pain and heartbreak of anything significant letting go to be something different. That's the thing about learning to let go. It is an act of Radical Faith to trust that whatever direction the river takes on the journey of the unknown is where our path was meant to take us. I had learned, however painfully with my best friend that sometimes boundaries have to be drawn. As my relationship with Anamchara ended, my best friend and I moved back to a place of friendship intimacy again. We started talking several times a day. She listened and supported my weight and my tears as I not only processed the loss of Anamchara but as I processed all the relationships that had come before him. She could help me remember those men, and who I was in my relationship with them. She could help me see the patterns of a lifetime of unconscious living. She was my mirror to the past. And in this journey, part of the healing was to look back and see the truth and then to be brave enough to say it out loud and let it go forever. My best friend was entering the place in her life of learning to let go as well. Her only child, my godson was turning 18 and leaving home and at the same time, her father, was dying of cancer.

My other soul friend showed up in my journey as the vision to the present and to the future. It's interesting to me that both of these women showed back up in my life to give me the mirrors I needed to see. I'd been friends with my lifeboat sister, as I've lovingly come to call her, since both of our boys were babies. We worked together shortly after I had delivered my son, while she was still pregnant with hers. She is the only person in my whole life that I have gone out of my way to be friends with. My lifeboat sister and I couldn't be more different, and thereby the same, from each other. She is salt of the earth and granola to the core. She is no shit, no games and no nonsense. On that, we are the same. It's an interesting dynamic to engage in a female relationship with someone who is as opinionated and forthright as you are yourself. With women, that can sometimes be a recipe for disaster. Not in our case, we can balance and hold each other up and know enough to step out of the way when necessary. I really don't know why in the beginning I was drawn to be her friend. Maybe that was the Universe setting us up for what would come eleven years later. It's hard to say. Our relationship journeys are completely different. Where men had a tendency to come and go in my life, she was the marrying kind. Throughout our whole friendship she had been with the same man, her husband. I believed they had the kind of marriage that would last forever. So did she. We were both wrong. As I took my journey with Anamchara, her marriage was coming to an end. She too, was learning the life lesson of letting go.

I would talk to both of my soul friends sometimes many times a day. They would listen patiently, offer profound wisdom and insight and simply hold the space for me to move through the River bound for letting go. I was able to do the same for both of them. We were able to have profound conversations about what it really means to be human, with human limitations, desires and fears. We sat in the middle of each other's pain and simply just let it rage. It was holding space for each other in a way of honor, truth, compassion and grace. We shared with each other the stark, naked truth of our humanness. And in being part of the others journey, the healing began in mine.

The interesting part of living the journey of letting go with my two soul friends was in the common threads of humanity that we shared when things come to an end. I believe as human beings we struggle against the tide of life in all beginnings and endings. It takes true Radical Faith to trust in a power higher than ourselves that there is a reason for our suffering. I really hate platitudes, those pithy little quotes that hang on the refrigerator to remind us of our common duality in being completely human. I came to live those platitudes and affirmations of life. They became my siren song to a life of opening up and letting go to the River that flows through all of us, the River of love, of joy, of creation of grief and loss. We all flow in the same river of consciousness. We are all one. The human experience is shared in its sameness of the experience. This is especially true in our ability to cope with grief and loss and learning to let go.

Often within hours, I would have the exact same conversation with both my lifeboat sister and my best friend for very different reasons. My conversations with one sister were always about seeking a higher spiritual truth and learning to leave behind a space that had grown too small. We talked often and at length about learning to let go, even when it's your choice to do so. Whether we make the choice, or it's made for us, the emotions are the same if we dig deep enough to feel them. We talked about sitting in the middle of our emotions and allowing them to move through us without balking and running away from their intensity. I'm still not sure either of us has found a way to do that gracefully.

There is this place I just call "the middle." It's that scary middle ground of knowing where you've been and what is now gone, but you have nothing yet to replace it. It's in that space, "the middle" that holds the most potential and opportunity for learning and spiritual growth. Every part of my body personality would rail at not having a definition for who I was or where I was going. My Wicked Ego Witch would use her most high pitched, ear splitting loud screams to try to get me to step back into the place of comfort that I'd just left behind, even when whatever I left behind was bad, it felt like a safer and more secure place than the terrifying space of possibility and the unknown. Trusting possibility and being ok with not knowing is my hardest challenge of them all so far. As my relationship with Anamchara ended I was left standing in my own grief and pain totally naked. I had no idea who I was going to be without him. I had no idea if I could remember all the lessons I'd learned along the way. I loved the person I was in his reflection. Who was I going to be standing on my own?

My conversations with my best friend were about learning to let go of roles. She was smack in the middle of watching her only child leave the nest and at the same time, watching her father die, far too young from cancer. Our conversations always revolved around the question, "Who am I supposed to be now?" For women in particular, I think this is a very difficult question to answer. So much of our lives are spent living up to, or down to, our father's expectations and in her case, this was particularly true. And then, just when we almost have that figured out, we become wives and mothers. Like it or not, I believe that those of us who choose to have children become defined by becoming a mother. I've come to believe, as much as I struggle against it, the role of mother to our children becomes our defining factor for most of our middle age. My role as mother became my sword and shield against participating in the world. For some of us, it is an excuse not to engage in our own spiritual growth and truth. In my case, this was particularly true. As we begin to watch our children and our parents leave us from their longstanding roles, we become faced with the unquestionable void their absence leaves behind. We learn about grief and loss from entirely different perspective. We are forced to stand in "the middle." We are forced to stand in our own truth of who we have allowed ourselves to become. And it is in this place we have the magical opportunity to call ourselves to come back home, where we've always belonged, standing strong in the center of our Truth.

My life coach gave me an amazing exercise that I still use today on a regular basis. It's called "Calling Home the Parts and Pieces of My Self." Along our journey, as relationships come and go, situations happen or don't happen, by choice or by force I believe we leave little pieces of ourselves behind. We give parts of our Self away to the world and in doing so, become fractionalized. Those pieces that say, "I will never kiss another man like that for the rest of my life." Those pieces that got told "You aren't good enough," or "You are not mother material," or whatever torrent the River of Life has washed into our lifeboat along the way. I learned from my life coach that I could call those pieces back to me. It's very simple actually. Picturing a large golden sun of consciousness and Divine Light shining above me I say simply, "I call all the parts of myself that I've given away, thrown away, got taken away or just lost along the way. I call all those pieces to come back home. It's safe and I need them now as a whole and conscious woman." I picture little rays of light coming from all across the expanse of the journey of my life returning home to me all those things I had lost.

I must admit, there was an essence of fear for me when I first started doing the exercise. I was terrified I was going to call back all those parts of me I'd worked so hard to lose. Those parts that got manic and crazy when a boyfriend disappeared, the parts of me that are irresponsible and unable to focus, those parts of me that are truly wild and just want to be free but here's the thing; when you call those parts and pieces back, they return under the supervision of your highest Truth. I'm a grown up now. I've learned the lessons (hopefully) that I needed to learn by walking those roads in the past. When my maniac returns, my adult steps in and says, "Really? Do you REALLY want to do THAT again?" The answer is always an internal smile and a very clear "No." Part of what was so powerful about my journey with my Anamchara is that the parts and pieces that returned to me were all the parts I love so much about myself. The passionate, sexual woman who isn't afraid of her own power returned. The loving, kind, supportive woman that is able to have a lifelong partnership with another returned. The little girl full of mischievous energy, passion and imaginative creation returned. Anamchara was the catalyst, the experience, but I did the work. He was just the mirror I needed to see so I could remember. It really was the journey to my own Divine Truth and calling back the parts and pieces of me that made the journey with Anamchara possible.

Together my soul friends and I would remind each other that we were not alone. That someone, somewhere – even if only connected by a phone line, someone could understand our pain and suffering. We were sharing our human experience and learning to dance in the naked truth of our call to grow more fully into ourselves as a result of our experiences. I learned from my friends that I was not alone, I was not unique and that the journey wasn't harder for me than for anyone else. There is incredible peace in that truth. When I sat alone and isolated in my grief, it become a nightmare. It become all there was. When I learned to share my story, and feel comfortable and supported in the weight of my own experience the load lightened and become more manageable along the way. I was learning how to speak my own truth and to give it its own voice. I was learning to expose my Wicked Ego Witch, and by doing so I learned I could minimize her voice.

My soul friends and I shared many laughs along the way which is simply Effortless Grace. To be able to laugh in the face of our stories of grief, rage and lack of control became the levity that enabled us to move through it with compassion and wisdom. Even for a pithy platitude, "Laughter is the best medicine" couldn't be more truthful in terms of learning to cope with the untenable nature of the River of life.

There were times that the Wicked Ego Witch would challenge me, and try to humiliate me into minimizing my loss of Anamchara against the losses of my soul friends. I mean really, I had such a brief relationship with this man, how could it possibly compare to the end of a long marriage that had produced a child or that child growing up and leaving home or worse yet, be compared to the truth that we all face, eventually we all watch our parents or someone else we love die.

The same weekend Anamchara and I ended our relationship another loss happened. One that is still so profound and unexplainable it's hard to write about. A few days into the worst of my personal grief I received a phone call of tragic proportion. When I owned my Ranch we were blessed to have a beautiful family living at the end of our driveway. A few months into living at the Ranch I finally realized that the man who lived in the house with his family was a former co-worker of mine. In fact, he worked at the same place I had met and worked with my lifeboat sister. He had a beautiful family, a wife he obviously loved more than life itself and two beautiful children. The oldest, his daughter, was the same age as my son. My son and his daughter would often play together in our woods. She was a beautiful, incredibly intelligent and charming little girl who would often say things so out of context and character for a child it would blow me away. On the same weekend Anamchara and I ended our relationship, this man's wife, and his daughter were killed when their car was destroyed by a man trying to escape police. His wife died at the scene. His daughter, my son's friend and playmate was taken from the scene by life-flight and died at the hospital when she arrived. In a moment, the fragile nature of life smacked me right in the face. Grief, loss and the precarious nature of being alive was right in front of me in a way I could never fathom for this man and the son that were left behind.

For as much as I felt my life had been changed forever by the loss of Anamchara, it became crystal clear to me that I was given a beautiful gift. He was still alive. The end of our story was not the kind of tragedy that happens every minute of every day in our world where people are taken from us, far before we're ready for them to leave.

My heart still aches for the man's loss. I can't imagine where his journey is taking him. But even in the face of this incredible tragedy, he has lessons to learn as well. I hope for him they are kind and gentle. At the funeral he wrote a letter which was read by a family member. The very last sentence of the letter touched me profoundly and even for its tragic origin was a grace note to me along the way. The last line was, "Love anyway…"

In the face of my own grief and loss, grace notes happened. They were those tiny little moments in time when I talked to a friend and could laugh. They were those moments when someone from my past showed up to say hello. Grace notes are the possibilities of life saying, stay true, feel what you feel and remember… if you're paying attention, the journey does continue.

Grace notes are the flowers that start to bloom in the spring, the warmth of the first summer day, the feel of the river cold and crisp when the temperature climbs over 100. Grace notes are the feel of my horse moving beneath me and the nicker of recognition when I walk up to the fence. Grace notes are every time my children smile and say, "I love you Mommy" and every time a sunset happens anyway after a day of rain. Grace notes are when the phone rings and you get to share a soul connection with another human on their journey. Grace notes are every unexpected life twist and turns that reminds us that no matter the loss that has passed behind us, a new adventure lies just ahead. Grace notes are getting to hold the space of your lifetime best friend as her father moved on from this lifetime and into another. Grace notes are every step that's taken into the future and saying yes to letting go. Grace notes make progress possible. With every grace note comes another possibility. I was learning to say yes to the grace notes. Every time I said yes, the grief lessened just a little bit and letting go became more and more possible.

Lessons learned…

I liken our human lifetime to being the River of Life. Each one of our human body personalities is given a perfect life boat that contains all we need for safe passage and learning the lessons we've come to this place to learn through our travels on the River. The life boat is our soul, our spiritual connection and Divine Truth. We all share the same River and have the beautiful privilege of sharing the journey with others who have made their way to the same point on the journey.

I can picture myself in the River of Life with all of my soul friends around me. The River is my journey, from birth to death. This story was just a brief section of my River, the stretch that led me to Heart Space. Along the way there were stretches of pure radiant sunshine and clear, calm effervescent water. And there were stretches of rapids that terrified me and challenged all of my strength and reserve to navigate. At different places along the journey I was caught up in a snag of rocks and my boat would beach. These were the twists in the River that supported my life lessons, the reasons I was taking this journey to begin with. Sometimes I spent a really long time pushing and pulling and fighting to release my boat just so I could get back to the River where I felt safe. Being stuck and feeling isolated and alone in a snag of rocks felt scary and uncomfortable. Mostly I spent enormous time and energy trying to muscle past the life lesson instead of taking the time it took to examine the problem and figure out the key to the lock of the lesson to release me. Sometimes it just took patience enough to wait for the River of Life to rise high enough to release me from the rocks all by itself. If I was too busy struggling and fighting and readjusting my boat, the tidal pull that happens naturally never had a chance to release me with its pure effortless grace of surrender.

Sometimes I unexpectedly jumped out of my lifeboat and right into the frigid cold water. Rugged individualism and just plain folly of being human made me forget that I had what I needed to safely navigate the waters. No, sometimes the lessons had to show up without any safety at all. It's those times where I disconnected from the spiritual truth of my Divine essence. I was all about the ego when I jumped into the water alone, the ego that says, "I can do this alone. I don't need any help at all." I was deaf to the Truth of who I was as a spiritual being. These lessons seemed to last the longest as I was battered between the rocks trying to find my own legs to stand upon. What

I failed to realize is that the lifeboat stayed beside me no matter how difficult the journey became beckoning me to climb back in to the safety and security of being in my own Divine Truth.

Sometimes, at just the right time, a soul friend would show up to give me a tug out of the snag if only I was willing to accept the outstretched hand offered in help and support. Sometimes I'd pull my boat over to a beautiful shore and share the respite of rest in relationship with another. Sometimes that relationship would lead to sharing the same boat for awhile. For as long as I could paddle in harmony with another, I could stay safely, together, in the boat of life. At other times, relationship struggles happening inside the boat made it too dangerous to continue, and the only course of action was to pull back over to the side and let the other person back out and into their own boat again. I've learned that it would take me awhile to figure how to navigate my boat safely because I'd gotten so comfortable with the other that I'd forget how to be all alone. Often they would leave pieces of their "stuff" in my boat which continued to bog down the smooth flow of my River. It's only when I was willing to toss the stuff they left behind into the River to be washed away, could I return to smoothly navigating the currents that were coming before me.

When I had children I learned that I tried desperately to attach their boats to my own, forgetting they have a soul journey of their own to take. Our tethered boats got bogged down as one boat snagged upon one rock, and another boat snagged against another. I didn't know that two separate boats, although tied together have different obstacles to overcome to get released from the snags. The longer I struggled against the flow of the their journey, the more difficult and fractured our journey became. Learning to parent gracefully is about letting our children navigate their own boats when its safe for them to do so, starting out in the calm and gentle waters and progressing to the rapids that will most certainly lay ahead.

It was hard for me to remember, when the storms of life happened, that my lifeboat was the very foundation of safety I need to pass through. I learned over time to hold on tightly as I would lose sight of the shoreline and begin to hear the roar of the waterfall just up ahead. With Radical Faith, and Effortless Grace I would drop to the floor of my boat, holding on to my paddles and let the journey and the River take me safely where it needs to go. I've learned that the easiest way to navigate the River is to go with its flow. Stay in its center and its balance trusting its promise of safe journey and passage if I would just stay out of the way.

Writing this story has been a journey all-together separate from what is being told on these pages. Looking back, and reflecting on where my River had been leading me, I could see the waterfall of dangerous rocks, sharp drops and low hanging tree branches that were scattered along the way. Many times I threatened to jump out of the boat, and sometimes I just did. I jumped out of my lifeboat when I bought the Ranch and ground myself into the oblivion of hard work and no empty spaces of spiritual truth where I could breathe. There were moments when I could sense the lifeboat was right there beside me, times like when I was guided to my Seer, to help me begin to open the spaces of expanded consciousness. Another happened when my animals surrounded me at the Ranch and helped hold my space of loss and grief in a way I'd never experienced before. There were moments on the early journey where I was starting to get a clue of the magical River all around me, moments when I would connect to the sacredness of the land that had called me to come, to heal and to start my journey of awakening.

Sorting back through the skeletons of my relationship closet I could see the brief glimmers of the hope and promise that had been contained in learning to love those that had come before the Anamchara of my heart. They had started the process of my life lesson to open my heart to all that was possible. I realized how many years of my life had been spent allowing the Wicked Ego Witch to captain my boat. Her screams of inadequacy had been my northern star of navigation by which I tried to safely find my way. I realized how much baggage of those relationships had been weighing down my lifeboat. It took much self-reflection and honest assessment to realize the time had come to release the baggage of others that had been left in my boat. There was no more freeing a moment than to see each of their pieces being tossed from my boat to float freely back into the River of Life. The Effortless Grace of being in my boat, alone in my Divine Truth is so much of what this tale has been written to tell.

    I learned about the soul friends along the way, that have always been in the River with me if I had only opened my eyes wide enough to just see them. Through the loving eyes of Radical Faith and Effortless Grace I finally said yes to the power and truth of sharing myself naked with the world around me. Sharing my humanity and learning and growing when they shared their humanity with me. I began to understand what it means to be fully present in each moment as it comes. That's still a difficult thing for me. I want to return to the past that I know so well and I want to live in a fantasy of hope for what might lie ahead. But, little by little, moment by moment I am remembering to stop reading my maps for the future or journaling the stories of the past to see the beauty of the banks of the River and all the beautiful souls traveling the journey with me. Radical Faith and Effortless Grace had always been right there with me, in their golden radiant glow. It was up to me now to honor their presence and give priority to their messages of Truth and healing.

    Profoundly I learned the beauty and the irony of traveling the journey on the River. I've learned that moments are transitory, and things always change. I now understand, albeit reluctantly and somewhat sadly, that each of us traveling this journey of life has our own boat to navigate. Agreements to travel the journey together sometimes last, and sometimes they don't. Learning to honor the unique journey of each of us is a particular challenge for me. It's in those times that I get banked on the rocks and struggle and fight. I jump out of my boat, leaving it beached on the rocks as I run screaming and shaking my fist at the sky in righteous indignation for how I thought things should have been. My boat waits patiently, and the tide of the River rises and I know, after I'm done shaking my fist, my boat will be waiting, already un-snagged from the rocks and ready to continue on down the River of Life.

Seeing and accepting the River of Life is seeing and accepting the expanded consciousness of Truth that is awakening all around us and within us. Beginning to see more than what can be explained is the part of the River that for me was fraught with scary twists and turns. Learning to stand in the middle of the fear of the unknown and learning to accept the Truths as they came is one of my greatest life lessons. Learning to trust my own expanded sight and the wisdom that comes directly from my soul is the part of the River I'm still learning to navigate. Sometimes it's easy, sometimes it feels impossible. I'm lucky that I was willing to open myself to the possibility of help along the way from my Seer. The work that we've done together so far, has given me the added push along the way to believe and trust in what was happening to me. My Seer was the teacher I needed to invite inside my lifeboat from time to time, to help me find my way. She helped to explain things my human personality didn't understand, things that my soul were so quietly trying to get me to see. Learning to trust my own Divine sight is still evolving. Having the experience of seeing the Warrior and his Bride was in truth, a bit shocking. It was so easy to dismiss. I am grateful that I had come to a place in my River where I was open to the possibilities of deeper learning of times and spaces for myself. Being privileged to have the experience of being shown my deeper truths is an honor I will never question again.

I learned about seeking... I learned so much about all the things I was packing around in my lifeboat as a desperate attempt to feel whole. I thought I needed all those things, all those experiences, all the change and chaos and confusion in my life. I finally figured out the weight I was carrying around was slowing down my journey and making it more difficult to navigate. There is no greater freedom, than standing in the simple, unadorned center, of my perfect lifeboat to take a breath in the beauty that surrounded me every single minute of every single day. When I threw all the distractions, baggage and chaos overboard, I was released from their bondage and was finally, free.

When the Dark Horse of Fear showed up in my journey, dancing wildly along the banks of my River I learned that I had choices. I learned that I could honor and respect her wisdom without jumping out of my lifeboat to join her on the shore. Fear had been such a living, breathing monster in my life that I had become completely unconscious of the tentacles and depth of her dark power. It was in fear that I shut myself off from the world and in fear that I refused to love. Anamchara was the reflection at the water's edge that I needed to see, about the Fear that I carried through my journey. Through his fear, I could so clearly see my own. And then I could see the Fear that radiates throughout humanity. It's in fear that we hide, in fear that we fight, it's in fear that as a race, the human race, we threaten to destroy our very home world. The Dark Horse began to challenge and illuminate in me those places that called to be healed. By rowing through the darkness, I found the light... the light of love, compassion, Radical Faith and Effortless Grace.

I learned far more than I lost in my relationship with my Anamchara. We had our lifeboats bound together for an epic journey to the center of ourselves. And on this journey, so much of my life became so clear. Most of the time in our relationship, I was jumping between his lifeboat and my own, back and forth. That was a real sign of growth for me. My relationship journeys before him were about jumping out of my lifeboat completely and jumping in with someone else. I gave up all knowing and truth for myself in those desperate times. I abandoned myself and my boat desperately hoping that the journey would be easier with someone else in control. I was wrong. I had left so much of myself in the boats of others, that it was a long scavengers journey to find all the pieces that had been dumped back into the River of Life by the souls I had left behind. But it was worth the effort. Tethered to him I found the pieces of my heart, pieces of my body, pieces of my passion and creativity and joy. He helped me by steering the boat so I could reach into the depths of the frigid River water to retrieve what I needed to bring back to the center of my own home. My Anamchara held safe emotional space, the space of kindred spirits and soul mates. He could hold on for me, because he understood me so well. He was who I needed him to be, so that I could learn the lessons I needed to learn. When our journey of romantic relationship came to an end, Anamchara did the only thing he would ever do. He reminded me with love and compassion to remember to take all my beautiful lessons with me as I returned to my own boat.

And I learned about letting go. I learned about all the endings that happen on the River, all the endings that make way, for new life. It's in the seasons of all things that the rich nuances of the journey on the River become so clear. It's in the end of relationships, the end of roles that define us, it's in the end of human life itself. If I would allow myself to be cast in the current of the storms that raged, eventually, the rainbows of Truth and Knowing would surround me. The time it took to find the rainbows doesn't mean they weren't already there waiting for me to notice. Letting go and moving on simply just takes as long as it takes. For me, there were so many detours along the way, detours because I got too tired to stay in the middle of the storm, so I pulled my lifeboat off for awhile simply to rest. There were detours because I was so angry, and so human that I kicked and screamed, begged and threatened to change the outcome. There were detours because I tried to find another way, a way that was easier than simply sitting through the middle, and hanging on until it was over. Sometimes Effortless Grace is honoring myself for just being exactly who I am, where I am and in the knowing that I can always change my mind and get back in the River to continue my journey, which is the choice that I finally made, for me.

The Seer...

As good fortune smiled upon me I was able to leave my regular life and fly off to the middle of America to return to my roots, to the place that calls my heart song of birth and tradition. I am a Kentucky girl at my very center. Shortly after I left Anamchara behind, still stuck in the middle of not knowing who I was to be without him, I got the opportunity to go back to the Midwest and visit old friends and family who remain there. Vividly I remember a moment in time as the trip was fast approaching where I said to myself and to the Universe, this was my chance. This was my golden opportunity to say yes to the unknown of possibility, stand in its shimmering center and let it unfold. This was to be new to me, always uncomfortable standing in a moment in time with the patience and fortitude to allow it to just be. But before I left, there was a phone call that I needed to make. The story was not yet told. So much had happened in my journey that I needed to see from a place of spiritual Truth. I felt different, I felt more centered and more whole but still caught in the unknown middle ground between body and spirit. What would The Seer tell me today?

6/13/09 "The image you're showing me is bright iridescent gold, like a candle flame tipped up to spirit. At the edge of the image is an aura of swirling energy all around you. You have done huge growth that has brought you to a place of being Spirit. This entire experience was about being connected to your spiritual truth. The question you now ask yourself is, "How do I live with that level of connected energy inside? You're clear in the center that you are not the energy and dynamics of the body. There is a shift in your "being-ness." You are learning to integrate the Spirit but the body is holding on to old patterns in a constricted space. It's time to clear those things."

Anamchara still weighed heavy on my heart and heavy in my mind. I needed to return to the space of relationship. I desperately wanted to hear the Seer say that something had changed or had shifted and that we were walking closer to each other instead of moving further away.

"I see two things. First is the two of you in the dance and flow of relationship. The second is the strong influence of other lifetimes. There is such a spiritual connection between the two of you. There is a profound depth that wants to pull you back into the old space. As you are living it, you remain clear that as this relationship currently is, it doesn't work – but it could." The Seer turned her attention Anamchara, and she said, *"He is starting to shift. He is still in the same place he was before, but energetically he feels the pull. He had ideas that constrict his reality that give him the information to say no to the possibility. He is not trusting his own power, he doesn't trust who he is as spirit. From a spiritual place the call to him is to unify himself. He doesn't trust that. He is starting to get more clarity that pieces of what he is doing aren't working anymore and he is unhappy and torn. You have this piece. You've done your work around it. For you the experience is, "Can you trust the experience from your deepest knowing?" You know what your truth of this is. Can you make peace with how*

it's unfolding?" That was the million dollar question and I didn't have an answer.

"As we begin to move and more fully integrate into our spiritual truth, the shift happens on a spiritual level immediately. What takes more time is waiting on the body personality to learn to trust a new way of being. The body works on linear time and sometimes the shift takes awhile, for the body learning to trust is something new."

I needed to have concrete answers. I needed a clear message that I could register, accept and live with. I asked my Seer, *"Is there anything more to the dance with this soul?"* She asked me, *"Do you feel anytime soon he's going to allow himself to do this piece of the work and, are you willing to support the time it takes for him to do this?"* There it was back at me. Rhetorical questions meant that I had to trust my own instinct and intuition to answer, but I suppose, that was the point. *"It doesn't feel complete to me."* I said in response. The Seer continued, *"The potential of this relationship is really attractive to him, but it lights all up the wounding places in him. If you are to continue it will require holding space for him to do the work in a subtle way. Don't take on the responsibility for him. Hold space for the possibility."*

There just wasn't anymore I could ask about Anamchara. As much as I wanted to kick and scream and beg for line in the sand answers, there just weren't any, and the frustration from that truth was mind bending. I wanted to call him, I wanted to drive down to see him, I wanted to tell him this truth and beg him to see – to see what I could see. The possibility of what we could have had together was so crystal clear to me and I believed that if he just knew the truth, he would be able to see it too and from there? The fairy tale, the happily ever after, the fireworks and the orgasms, the laughter, joy and huge diamond rings I had sold myself on. And there the fantasy ended. It was so much simpler to be stupid. It would have been easier to be ignorant of the spiritual truth and knowing of things, a truth so clear that even if I wanted to ignore it, and believe me I did, and I do, there wasn't anything I could do about it at all. I was going to have to play the biggest poker hand of my life. I was going to have to wait and trust and believe. I was going to have to trust that I would know when to lay down my hand or when to just fold and walk away.

The Seer and I left relationship space and moved on to other spaces in my life, because contrary to my own beliefs, Anamchara and the relationship was only a tiny fraction of who and what I am. This journey for me was about opening my own heart space, finding my own connection to spirit and living more fully into who I am supposed to be in this world. *The Seer said, "The project you're working on lights up your heart chakra, your female creative energy is filled with passionate juiciness. Your challenge remains in this area, like other, to trust spirit and to help move the body personality more in line. This is a huge shift in your awareness and that's why we're here. You have curiosity and frustration for not knowing. Use self love, compassion and trust in the process. Trust what comes up for you. Put your faith and trust in that what is here and that what is coming, is a continuation on your path."*

So there it was. Trust myself with love and compassion. Yikes.. was I ready? The body personality and the Wicked Ego Witch puffed up to roar their hideous roars. The next couple of days I went back and forth. I mean really, what kind of idiot could I possibly be? Anamchara had walked. I'd had that happen before and I'd believed silly idealisms of fateful reunions that never happened —well, actually historically speaking, they always did happen, I've never been in a relationship where the other didn't return at some point on the continuum and the end result was always the same as the original version... goodbye. This was not history I wanted to repeat. There was no reason to walk down that mired road of misery again with Anamchara. I swirled in self-doubt and innuendo. I danced a thousand dances between body and spirit. My body and ego clear that I was making all this up to suit myself. Anamchara was not going to return and that my "knowing" was simply a fantasy I'd built to make myself feel better in the end. In those quiet moments between ego ranting, Radical Faith was still whispering, "Stay open, believe."

The Seer and I rallied a couple emails back and forth where I was desperately, however ill concealed, tried to get her to be more clear about the destiny of my relationship with Anamchara. It became pretty clear, pretty quickly that I was still stuck. I was really hoping when I called her for the second time in three days that she would tell me the abject truth that we were just over and my body personality was just holding on.

6/16/09 - "Your spiritual awareness is wider than your body knowledge and it's trying to pull you into knowing about your relationship. On a soul level, the intention was growth, your own healing and growth. You mind is challenging and trying to figure out what this knowing means. It does get easier as your body personality gives way to what spirit knows as Truth. The body is what is making you question. Trust that Divine beings are guiding you in perfect time. Trust yourself and trust spirit." I asked the Seer the one question I desperately needed to have a clear answer about, "What piece of information does my spirit want me to know about this relationship?" And I held my breath as she answered, so sure I already knew the answer, "TRUST LOVE," and she giggled and said, "You might want to share that with him." She went on to say, "There is a great love between you. Trust the love you have for each other. You are both working on elements of Trust. You each have your own version. You are both learning to trust yourselves in different ways. He wants to be with you, he just doesn't know how to do it. He doesn't believe it's possible. Allow yourself to be in the energy and go with its flow. This has been a pivotal process for you that is shifting your whole stance of yourself. It's a challenge. You're learning how to do this and keep your personal balance."

I was floored and practically speechless. What was the point of going all the way around the bush to come to the answer I had always believed to be true – that I had to trust myself and Anamchara to do what we need to do? When my relationship with him ended and I talked to the Seer who revealed all our past life history with each other, why didn't this come up? What did trust love mean? My body personality wasn't going to be satisfied with platitudes.

I asked the Seer about future possibility agreements between Anamchara and me. "When I see possibilities I see threads connecting all over the Universe of possibility. There is a way in which the body personality looks at and judges possibility – what you believe to be possible. It's like you can focus only on ten possibilities, nine of which are safe so you put most of your energy there. Give equal space to ALL possibility all the millions of possibilities. They all exist. Where you put your energy either negatively or positively affects the potential and the outcome of the possibility. You could have your dream manifest or EVEN MORE. It is a possibility, but again, hold equal space for all possibility on the continuum. He has his part to play in this dynamic. Trust love in the context of this dance. Have hope in the actual dynamic. Own fully all the spaces of possibility. You are learning how to be proactive in your choices, focus your intention on your life. You are learning to have images in your life without them becoming your life. Some possibilities you will hold expanded space for and make choices towards. It becomes a conundrum. Your body says, wait a minute, I don't know how to do this, but you do. Trust Radical Faith and the manifestation of Effortless Grace. Don't engage any of the dynamics simply hold space and trust. Each person has to learn how to do this for herself. There is a flow between body and spirit. On one hand, it's easy, on the other hand, it isn't easy at all. Really look at and be clear about your intentions. That is when the lessons stop repeating. I needed to ask another question, because it's what I do when I'm not 100% clear about the answers or if I am hoping that I'll hear something different than I've already heard. I asked the Seer, "What does he really want me to know – from spirit?" She answered, "That he really is trying. He's still in the dark room and can't find the door. He's still entrenched in body personality. He doesn't know what to do. There is a strong tension there, a strong drive from spirit to do this piece of the work. His spirit is looking down on his body. This dynamic is unconscious to him at this time. Your role in this dynamic is to hold the space of possibility but don't do the work for him. Be benevolent and compassionate. Trust Divine timing because you're not done with it. Trust the process, work on your parts of it and hold space for all possibilities. There is a natural rhythm to all things. Find some amusement and lightness in this dynamic. In the midst of the challenges, ask, where is my lightness?"

And as we hung up the phone, Effortless Grace surrounded me. As I breathed in her grace, I felt Radical Faith pick up her sword and shield to protect me and give me the strength to move on.

Of all the things the Seer and I had talked about throughout this journey, the one that really hit home immediately was holding equal space for ALL possibilities, and with that visceral realization I could get on the airplane bound for another adventure and say yes to what was coming ahead.

The Space of Possibility…

When the plane landed in Kentucky I was filled with nerves and the tenuous threads of learning what it means to be out of control, at the mercy of those around me and simply going with the flow of where the River was taking me. I walked down the gangway, out through security and into the open arms of a man I hadn't seen in 25 years. Giddy with the excitement of the new and unknown I flew into his arms and allowed myself to take a breath there. They were the arms of another. We laughed, sang, danced and found solace in each other for the few hours we had together again. I allowed myself to be swept off my feet and rode the tide of pleasure and companionship with another. I allowed myself the precious treasure of being treated like a princess of possibility in his eyes and the truth be told, together we found a spark of passion neither of us would have said out loud was realistic or likely. Our time together was short lived, and insignificant except for its context to me. To me it was permission to stay open and move on when the right man and the right time comes along. It was the gentle and kind Universe saying someday, you will love again, if not with the Anamchara, then with another.

As we returned to his home climbing out of his truck, I opened my eyes in the childish wonder of my little girl. Scattered all over the sidewalk as if to say, "Yes, this is just for you," was the most brilliant display of iridescent light and hopeful illumination into the magical world of lightning bugs. My hands flew to my mouth and squeals of delight escaped my lips to the amusement of those around me. Jumping up and down and running around wildly I found myself at eight years old again trying to catch these beautiful bugs with their ethereal presence in the soft open palms of my hands. I wanted to fill a mason jar, as I'd done so many times in my childhood with these precious treasures and keep them forever on my shelf of life memories to remind me to honor my little girl and allow her to play. But with the wisdom that comes with the journey I finally understood that the magic was in being completely present in the moment. So I left them there, to fly free and unrestricted in life, as I keep their memory shining brightly in the center of my very open heart.

It was the start to what would be a grand adventure of letting go and having life say yes, stay open, it's worth it. Trust all possibilities. I spent time doing all the things I love best in the world. Horses, music, food, family and yes, even shoes. The world was my oyster on these few days away from home. A beautiful sunny beach of respite and reward for the journey I had traveled. I had learned to relax and open up and take each moment for what it was in front of me. As the rest of my trip unfolded, the magic and possibilities continued. One adventure bled into the next as I simply just stayed in the center and let it be. It was without question, and without proper explanation, the most incredible "end" to a journey that could have been.

As the plane made its descent back to my home and to my children I was able to see with the keen hindsight and illumination of reflection on the journey I had been taking since I bought the Ranch. I had said yes. To the Dark Horse of fear I said, "Let's ride." To the joy I said, "Let it sweep me away." To my little girl I said, "Time to play." To my woman I said, "I honor and respect you." To the adventure I said, "I am ready." To my Anamchara I said, "Thank you. Thank you for being who I needed you to be so that I could learn what I needed to learn." To my children I said, "I am ready to show you the real me." To the sameness and difference of each day I said, "I am present." To the sorrow I said, "Let me feel." To the beginnings I said, "I am willing." To the ends I said, "I am sad and I'm willing to sit in the space of sadness and simply be." To the possibilities that remain ahead I said, "I am open and willing." To myself I said, "Welcome home."

As I stepped off the plane and back into my life one thing was absolutely certain. My life is forever and completely changed as a result of the experiences and journey that had led me to this place. I walked back into my life full of all the lessons that had been so recently revealed to me. With Radical Faith and her absolute clarity in the journey firmly in control of my helm and Effortless Grace with her peaceful conviction calming the waters before me, the Ego Witch is now quiet, at least my Heart Space. She's lost the piercing shrill of lies masqueraded as the truth she told for so long inside my head. In some ways we've made peace, the Witch and I. I understand her to be an aspect of who and what I am. She has important things to say from time to time, and it's up to me from my place of Spirit to listen with the discerning ear of wisdom and truth. As I settle in for the next journey I find my own voice, the Warrior inside me is abundant, resounding and strong as I fill my lungs with the cool river air and simply say yes to the River of Life and where the journey is taking me next.

Epilogue...

There is always more to every story, for as long as the lessons and healing need to take for us to get what we were meant to get in the first place. Every waterfall has a beginning and an end, but the path of the water stays in a continuous flow leading us forward to the next journey on the path to our Divine Truth.

When I saw him again, my Anamchara, I believed that our journey of relationship had given way to something different, something that would have kept our journey of souls together in the flow. I was wrong. When I saw him again he was different. Something had changed, or perhaps it was me who had changed and because of the distance and the view I could see him for his Truth. I could see all the facets of what it means to be human. It all became so clear. Anamchara, in our journey together through Heart Space was the mirror that I needed him to be. What I saw in him was a reflection of myself – all the beautiful, strong, loving things that were buried so deeply inside of me. He was the key to the lock to open the chains and I let him. I found the courage to look in the mirror he held up for me to find myself. He came to lead me to the place of the heart—where love for myself and for all things reside. It's a space of beauty, grace and passion. I said yes, that was my journey.

In our soul agreement with each other I was to be his Anamchara as well. I was to teach him as many things as he was to teach me. I came to lead him to Spirit, to the center of himself, to the place of Divine Truth that resides in us all. I don't honestly know where he is on his journey because he is no longer a part of my life. He had his own lessons and reactions to the Heart Space we found together. Now when I think of him, I am overcome with gratitude and appreciation for the simple knowing of our lifetimes of learning together, doing the same dance of karma over and over again. I hold him in my newly open heart with grace, compassion and love. I let him go to follow his River of Life without me.

As I wave goodbye, I sink to my knees in the floor of my boat. Radical Faith whispers quietly as she slips her arms around my neck with the promise and hope in the journey of what is to come. Effortless Grace bathes me in sunlight as she wipes away my tears of what might have been. In the light of grace I notice the water lapping quietly against a beautiful sandy beach. I hear the whiny in the distance, and there, in the magnificent shimmering light stood Satori. As she rose out of the sand and came into her full height she transformed inside the depths of my own knowing to become magnificent white. Satori is intuitive illumination - the keys to the kingdom and I was ready to ride her with Radical Faith, Effortless Grace and the wisdom that had been inside me all along.

I climbed out of my lifeboat and jumped both feet into the shallow shoreline of the beach as Satori stood waiting for me. As my last foot left the water's edge I felt a familiar and seductive hand wrap itself around my ankle. The Wicked Ego Witch begged me to return to my senses of fear and control. I shook her off, knowing she would always be a part of me in this human lifetime. I smiled down at her, honored her for her place and kept walking forward. Satori went down to her knees to allow me to climb onto her illuminescent back. With my hair wound into her flowing mane, and my thighs pressed into her belly, we took flight into the magic and promise of the moment.

About the Author

JULIE JACOBS lives in the Pacific Northwest with her two children, Saint Bernard and two horses, Dixie and Legacy. A passionate horse enthusiast with a gift for helping woman overcome their fears, she is embarking in the world of Equine Assisted Psychotherapy. Currently working on her second book, "With Radical Faith and Effortless Grace… Here and Now" Julie is looking forward to her next journey with the Seer, her four-legged soul friends and the others that show up along the way. She can be reached at www.radicalfaith-effortlessgrace.com

About the Cover Artist:

KIM McELROY is renowned for her equine art. For over two decades her pastels have graced popular greeting cards and collectibles, pastel originals and fine art prints. Her visions of horses portray the power and beauty of the horse's form and offer us a timeless glimpse of its soul. The horse is her muse, and she is always seeking new ways of expressing elements of the horse's spirit in a quest to awaken humanity to their healing gifts.

Kim is co-creator and illustrator of the "Way of the Horse ~ Equine Archetypes for Self-Discovery " Book and Card Set by Linda Kohanov, and author and illustrator of the "Way of the Horse Journal"

Kim lives on a farm with her husband Rod, six horses and a menagerie of creatures in Kingston, Washington Her websites are: www.spiritofhorse.com: and www.spiritof-horsecards.com

"Julie's invitation to create the cover for this book began my own journey into "Radical Faith and Effortless Grace". Julie's support of my intuitive and artistic process made it a pleasure to envision her creation. Then only a brief time after we began our plans, she found out we'd need to have the artwork done in a matter of weeks! I launched into the creation of the painting, and surprised even myself at the ease and flow with which the creation expressed itself. I know this had a lot to do with the energy behind her wonderful book, and the intent of her message of love. May Faith and Grace inspire you to embrace your own potential…"

~ Kim McElroy

Purchasing "Leap of Faith"

Kim and I are pleased and proud to offer "Leap of Faith" as a package purchase option. For $39.95 you can receive a signed copy of "*With Radical Faith and Effortless Grace... Journey to Heart Space*" and a 6.5 x 10 poster of "Leap of Faith".

Other "Leap of Faith" purchase options include:

Size	Type	Price	Shipping
6.5 x 10	Poster	$30.00	Shipping 7.00
9 x 14.5	Poster	$60.00	Shipping 10.00
12.5 x 20	Poster	$95.00	Shipping 12.00
16.5 x 26	Poster	$135.00	Shipping 12.00
19 x 30	Poster	$175.00	Shipping 12.00
6.5 x 10	Giclée	$65.00	Shipping 10.00
9 x 14.5	Giclée	$125.00	Shipping 20.00
12.5 x 20	Giclée	$200.00	Shipping 30.00
16.5 x 26	Giclée	$275.00	Shipping 35.00
19 x 30	Giclée	$350.00	Shipping 40.00

All Giclée prints are signed by Kim McElroy. All artwork will be shipped directly by Kim McElroy and will arrive separately from the book.

Posters versus Prints

Kim McElroy's Custom Giclée Prints are made to order by her printmaker at Digital Canvas Northwest, using the highest quality Epson printers and archival inks tested at 200 years, printed on an exquisite German Etch 100% rag watercolor paper. The texture of this paper lends makes the print look like an original pastel. The technique of this printing allows for a beautiful reproduction of the image because there is no detail lost in the fine spray of the printing pigments.

The sizes listed are the image size. The prints are surrounded by a 1" white border and are hand-titled and signed by the artist in pencil in the border, and come with a Certificate with the story behind the art.

Packaging
Depending upon the print size and shipping requirements, prints are usually shipped flat and are mounted attractively on white paper, backed with cardboard, and enclosed in a protective mylar sleeve for ease of viewing and handling until they can be framed.

Shipping
Because the prints are made to order -- please allow 1-2 weeks for us get your print in house -- to inspect, sign, and ship it. Expedited shipping is available upon request.

Archival Poster Prints
Kim's Custom Poster Prints are made to order by her printmaker at Digital Canvas Northwest, using the highest quality Epson printers and archival inks tested at 200 years, printed on a lighter weight matte finish paper. The sizes listed are the image size. The prints have a ½" border and are not hand signed.

Packaging
These prints are shipped rolled in a tube.

Shipping
Because the prints are made to order -- please allow 1-2 weeks for us get your print in house -- to inspect, sign, and ship it. Expedited shipping is available upon request.

This artwork is available for purchase through my website:
www.radicalfaith-effortlessgrace.com

INDIGO MOON PUBLISHING
Portland, OR
www. radicalfaith-effortlessgrace.com